John 5:19

JAY W. WEST

2013

Endorsements

"Encouragement, Biblical teaching, true-life stories, and mind-set challenges are all involved in Jay West's book, *Downloads from Heaven*. I love Jay's conversational style of writing that should draw in every reader. It can be a strange concept to some to think that we, mere humans, could actually hear from God and receive His direction, instructions, and knowledge. Yet, Jay makes a clear case that the Bible does teach exactly that truth and that each follower of Christ can experience a word of knowledge from the Holy Spirit as a regular part of life.

In *Downloads from Heaven*, Jay lays the Biblical foundation for his premise, and then follows up with story after story of personal encounters that illustrate the Biblical truth. People love stories! And Jay West's personal stories are fun *and* funny - a great way for everyone to see the simplicity of the gifts of the Spirit. I love how Jay takes the "spookiness" out of walking in the Spirit that some Christians have been taught. This book clearly demonstrates the beautiful New Testament reality that every believer is a candidate to hear from and act upon a word straight from their Father's heart to theirs. I believe *Downloads from Heaven* will be the launching pad for a new infusion of faith for believers to experience, and then release to others, a tangible, loving message from the Heavenly Father that brings life and changes lives for the glory of Christ!"

Pastor Kristen Gray
Missionary to Cuba & Latin America
Great Door Ministries
www.greatdoorministries.org
Omaha, NE

"Does God still speak to His people? Do you want to know how, when and where? Then *Downloads from Heaven* is a book you want to read. Jay West documents Scripture in a masterful way and exposes strategies and tactics meant to keep us from understanding how God communicates with His people today. The systematic methodologies explained by Jay will make an indelible impression and lead people to a greater understanding of how the Lord still communicates to and through us. Jay's style of writing and personal testimonies are down-to-earth, funny and real without being weird or scary. This book is for every believer and a must-read for those who want to learn to know God's voice."

James K. Hart
Lead Pastor, Eagle's Nest Worship Center,
Omaha, NE

"*Downloads from Heaven* is exciting and captivating yet simple and fun to read. It is easy to read yet it presents a foundational truth. This may sound like heresy, but I believe most Christians put too much emphasis on the written Word or Logos Word (the Bible) and far too little emphasis on the Rhema Word or Living Word (the Holy Spirit). This book shows how receiving downloads from heaven (Living Word) can cease from being occasional events and can become a process or a way of living with the Living Word. It is as simple as saying, "Yes Lord" to every slight nudge of the Holy Spirit.

Jesus spent 3 years mentoring the disciples 24/7 and answering their questions, but He told His disciples it was good that He was leaving them because He would send them something better, which was not a book. He was going to send the Holy Spirit to His followers which meant they could get continuous Downloads from Heaven.

When I met Jay 30 some years ago, he was already practicing getting downloads from heaven. So this is not just a theory but a way of life for Jay. He is showing you how it can be a way of life for you. I am in complete agreement with Jay that downloads from heaven needs to be a way of life for us. Jesus said the Holy Spirit would teach us all things. I personally have been practicing this as a way of life for more than 81 years.

Jay begins the book with a dilemma. He hears an internal voice say, "Get off this plane! It is going to crash!" What should he do? Get off the plane and let the others die? Ignore the voice? What would you do? You need to read quite a ways to discover what Jay did."

Dr. Neil Kanning, Pastor
Previous scientist who designed
the shape of the Space Shuttle

"*Downloads from Heaven* is an inspiring and often entertaining account of what the Lord is doing through the ministry of Jay West."

Gary Peterson, MA,
Assistant Professor and Chairman,
Humanities Dept. Grace University, Omaha, NE.

DOWNLOADS

FROM HEAVEN

Jay W. West

For further information, to book Pastor Jay West, or to order resources:

Please contact us at by email at anointed2go@cox.net
or online at www.anointed2go.com.

Dedication

I thought I would take a different course with my dedication page by selecting someone that I have never met, but someone whom I have read about, and probably so have you.

This fellow made a lot of mistakes, but he ended up being a great preacher, evangelist, and yes, even an apostle. In his early days he seemed to be bungling lots of kingdom ministry, but he later proved to be a valuable asset to God and to the cause of Christ. I think we can all see a little bit of ourselves in this man's early years as a follower of Jesus.

And believe it or not, this guy was actually called *blessed* by Jesus.

Now, it is one thing for you and I to be called *blessed* by someone that we know or have met, but it is quite another thing to be called *blessed* by Jesus. That was awesome, cool, and sweet all together.

So, I dedicate this book to the Apostle Peter, who received one of the first New Testament Words of Knowledge; or in modern day vernacular, "a download from heaven," as outlined in Matthew 16:13-19.

Peter, you illustrated true discipleship by having listening ears and a teachable heart. I so appreciate your tenacity and willingness to grow in your faith and learn from the Master. Thanks for being faithful and for setting the bar up high for the rest of us to follow. Dude, you done good.

Acknowledgments

Wow—where do I start? First, to my lovely, kind, and patient wife, Diane, I offer a profound and heartfelt "Thank you." I cannot count or tell you the number of times you said to me, "You should write a book." And it's not a secret either (smile). But after so many newsletter articles, magazine submissions, Bible studies, and email blogs came the encouraging words, "You should write a book." Thanks for helping me believe it was possible. Thanks for loving me through the process. And thanks for saying "yes" so many years ago, making this first acknowledgement so special to me. Lou ya.

Okay, Jason Bradley West. I won't tell the world your many other middle names, but if I did, it would include, "You can do this, Daddy." You have worked so hard on this book from the beginning when I first began to write, to helping me with chapter titles, plus the first edit, to formatting, along with set-up and design, including ordering ISBN numbers, and hours and hours of computer technology that made my job so much easier. I could never have done this without you. Wow! Let me write it backwards. Wow! Love, Pastor Daddy.

Other people that I want to thank in random order are:

Cynthia Pleskac, for patient hours of cover design and then discovering I had accidentally given you the wrong format to follow. You are a gem!

Gary Peterson, who provided the second edit, but prior to that, on many occasions, suggested to me that I write a book. Also, thank you for writing one of the recommendations and actually using your real name, and not your pen name. Gary, you are a blessing to the faculty at Grace University.

Pastor Duaine Johnson, Senior Pastor of Purpose Church, for your time and encouragement to help us just after you wrote your first book. God bless you and Latosha as you plant this new church in St. Louis, MO. Let me know when you switch from tea to coffee.

Pastor Keith Grimm, for writing the foreword, and for inspiring me to live for Jesus in an uncompromised way. Too bad you can't play pool as well as you preach, but we all have a cross to carry (LOL).

Pastor Kristen Gray, for writing a recommendation and for your encouragement from the first time we came to the Nest, to actually inspiring Pastor Hart to read my book in advance of it being printed. Do you know how amazing that is? He did not read Pastor Duaine Johnson's book until after it was printed.

Dr Neil Kanning, you have been a friend from the day I met you in Bradenton, Florida, to now. I will never forget your hospitality in Columbus, Ohio; your visit to Omaha, Nebraska; and your many phone calls and emails to encourage and pray for me. Your authorship of one of the recommendations is priceless. But next time I come to your house, please don't hide that larger bed from me.

Pastor Hart, Lead Pastor at Eagle's Nest Worship Center in Omaha, I have learned so much sitting under your anointed teaching and inspiring messages. You honored me by letting me share words of knowledge from when we first began attending to now. Thanks for trusting me to preach, to share with Ignite and with the children, and for giving me a lot of freedom to minister elsewhere. I am grateful for your kindness towards our family in so many wonderful ways, including the time you picked them up from the accident scene during a heavy snowstorm and took them home. Now that your wife has been asked to write a book, it may be time for you to launch out in this realm too.

Finally, to God: Thank you for the Spiritual Gift of words of knowledge. I'd write more, but you already wrote the Book! Mine is just the sequel.

Contents

Foreword

The Holy Spirit doesn't want to be the toy that we occasionally play with and then put back on the shelf. His passion is to transform all of us into Christ-centered, Spirit driven, kingdom minded, and constantly available servants. By God's grace, this is exactly what Jay is. Standing six feet six inches in height, Jay is tall in stature. Yet his heart for discipleship, Christian education, healing, compassionate care and mobilizing people for mission is even bigger.

You are going to love this book. But if you knew Jay personally, you would love him even more. Whether hanging out, watching football, building fences, trimming trees, playing pool, socializing as families, or ministering together, Jay's friendship and loyalty have always been vital to me.

His practical and pointed teaching, bold witness, joyous heart, sacrificial lifestyle and incredible testimony of a life healed and radically used by Jesus Christ will inspire you.

No matter what circumstances you face or what conditions you are currently enduring, the Holy Spirit longs to be downloaded into your life. When He is, look at what Christians become...

- Fishers of men, faithful, pure in heart, peacemakers;
- Sons of God, salt of the earth, lights of the world, wise;
- Righteous, merciful, patient, pleasing to God;
- Holy, harvesters, healers, hopeful;
- Servants, cross bearers, witnesses, saints;
- Freed from sin, unafraid, unashamed, more than conquerors;
- Children of God, joyful, accepting, all things to all people;
- Living sacrifices, blameless, God's temple, the body of Christ;
- Citizens of heaven, trusting, protecting, immovable;
- Comforters, new creations, compassionate, crucified with Christ;
- Thankful, bold, generous, ambassadors of Christ;
- God's workmanship, forgiving, understanding, kind;
- Quick to listen, slow to speak, slow to anger, victorious;
- Doers of the Word, rooted in love, impartial, and belonging to God forever.

As you read this book, rejoice in who you are in Christ and what He has already done for you. Then ask the Holy Spirit to continuously download His wisdom, grace and gifts to expand the kingdom of God in and through your life.

To God alone be the glory!

Keith Grimm
Senior Pastor of Beautiful Savior
Lutheran Church in La Vista, Nebraska

Preface

When you think of the word *download*, what comes to mind? Most people immediately think of computers and technology. And rightly they should, for that is where the term originated. However, it is not often that people think of downloads that come from heaven. What does a download from heaven look like in practical, everyday life? That is what you will soon discover as you read this book!

Many people get the terms "download" and "upload" confused. Yet, the difference is really quite simple. A download is information that is sent from a larger computer system to a smaller computer system; whereas, an upload is information that is sent from a smaller computer system to a larger computer system.[1] If you think of these terms as they relate to the heavenly realm, downloads from heaven involve hearing from God, and uploads to heaven involve praying to God. In this book, you will hear many personal examples from my father of how he personally downloaded information from God and uploaded information to Him on a regular basis. Truly, hearing from God and prayer go hand-in-hand. You really cannot have one without the other.

As we pray, one of the most important things we can do as believers is to have a hearing heart. In fact, King Solomon asked for this very thing when the Lord appeared to him in a dream. In 1 Kings 3:9a, he said, "Therefore give to Your servant an understanding heart to judge Your people." The footnote in my Bible says that the literal translation of "an understanding heart" is a "hearing" heart. Of course, we know what happened next in verse ten: "The speech pleased the Lord, that Solomon had asked this thing." God is very pleased when we want to have hearing hearts. After all, the opposite of a hearing heart is a hardened heart. And a hardened heart leads to rebellion. Psalm 95:7b-8a says, "Today, if you hear His voice: 'Do not harden your hearts, as in the rebellion.'"

I believe that hearing from God is directly related to wisdom. Solomon asked for a hearing heart, and as a result, God gave him a "wise and understanding heart" (1 Kings 3:12). As believers, the more we learn how to hear from God, the more we will be able to live with a lifestyle of wisdom and discernment. My charge to you, the reader, is this: Before you go any further in reading this book, ask God to give you a hearing heart for what he would have to say to you throughout the text. As you read these inspiring and convicting teachings and stories, do not harden your heart. Rather, listen to what God would tell you. Get ready to embark on a journey of learning how to hear God's voice and how to apply His instructions to the circumstances around you. Get ready to receive downloads from heaven!

Jason B. West, age 20
Sophomore at Grace University, Omaha, NE
Worship Leader and Songwriter, Anointed 2 Go MdM

Crash?

As a traveling minister, I spend a great deal of time in airports. Years ago, while traveling through a certain Midwestern city, I was waiting for my connecting flight in an unfamiliar airport. As I was waiting, I heard a voice inside my head saying, "Don't get on the plane—it's going to crash." The voice kept repeating inside of me, saying not to get on the plane because it was going to crash.

I began to scan the airport waiting area, looking for a Christian who could pray with me. But if there were any around, they weren't blowing their cover. I am sure you have heard of people who got a premonition that something terrible was going to happen, so they changed their plans at the last minute and averted a disaster.

Here I was in this terminal having these thoughts. At that point, I wondered: Why do they call these places *terminals*? The people on my plane were beginning to board the aircraft, and the voice was getting louder: "Don't get on the plane—it's going to crash! Don't get on the plane—it's going to crash!" As I was walking down the jet-bridge, it actually felt more like a gangplank. I literally thought I might die and never see my family or friends again. What should I do? I was truly having a critical moment of decision.

I will finish this story in a later chapter, explaining how I decided to discern the voice and understand my role in God's Kingdom. However, it is important for us to know that God does want to talk to us. John 10:27 clearly articulates this when Jesus speaks and says, "My sheep hear My voice, and I know them, and they follow Me." He wants us to listen to His voice too.

In Revelation 3:20, we read more of Jesus' words when He says, "Behold I stand at the door and knock. If anyone hears My voice and will open the door, I will come in to him and dine with him, and he with Me." Most of us knock with our hand or ring the doorbell with our finger. But according to this verse, Jesus knocks with His voice. Jesus is calling—will we listen? Jesus is calling—will we open the door? Jesus is calling—will we respond to His voice?

This book is filled with personal stories of times I heard God speak, along with the results that came from responding to His promptings. Throughout the book, I will also share some definitions and biblical illustrations that will help solidify the stories and examples. Finally, I will provide some practical advice and prayers that will assist you as you grow in your ability to hear the voice of God.

If you have a desire to download more messages from Heaven than you have in the past, then you are reading the right book. If you want to grow in your understanding of how God talks to us, then keep reading. And if you truly want to move in the gifts of words of knowledge, wisdom, and discernment, then prayer-fully seek the Lord while you continue reading.

Chapter 1

Teaching

As I begin this book with you, it is important that we take a moment to lay some foundational teaching on exactly what a word of knowledge is and how a word of knowledge is downloaded from God. To do this, we need to look at some Scripture in the Bible. We will begin in Matthew 16:13-19:

> When Jesus came into the region of Caesarea Philippi, He asked His disciples, saying, "Who do men say that I, the Son of Man, am?"
>
> So they said, "Some *say* John the Baptist, some Elijah, and others Jeremiah or one of the prophets."
>
> He said to them, "But who do you say that I am?"
>
> Simon Peter answered and said, "You are the Christ, the Son of the living God."
>
> Jesus answered and said to him, "Blessed are you, Simon Bar-Jonah, for flesh and blood has not revealed this to you, but My Father who is in heaven. And I also say to you that you are Peter, and on this rock I will build My church, and the gates of Hell shall not prevail against it. And I will give you the keys of the

kingdom of heaven, and whatever you bind on earth will be bound in heaven, and whatever you loose on earth will be loosed in heaven."

Please notice that Jesus asked a simple question regarding what others are saying about Him, and He received a variety of answers. But Peter answered the question correctly. Jesus responded to that answer by stating that Peter did not get that information from anyone around him, nor did Jesus even teach it to him, but rather it was given to Peter as a direct word of knowledge from the Father in Heaven. This was a download from heaven.

So we see a spontaneous yet accurate word of knowledge that was shared with Peter from God. But Jesus went on and added that Peter is equated to a rock, and that strength and stability started to come to Peter. A sign of good discipleship is when people are solid in their approach to ministry and to the faith that they have received in Jesus. As Paul says in Ephesians 4:14-15, they are no longer tossed about by every wind of doctrine, but rather, they are in a sure place with a sure foundation and sure footing. Jesus was imparting this aspect to Peter.

Jesus also calls Peter "blessed." Wow, it doesn't get much better than this. It's one thing to call yourself blessed, or to have someone else say that about you; but when Jesus calls you blessed, you know you are blessed! And I know that there are probably many definitions for *blessed*, but the one I like goes like this: Blessed—empowered to prosper and be in control of situation, regardless. That is an incredible stance and posture to have in your possession. Wow!

And not only did Jesus impart blessing to Peter, but He gave him and others authority with the keys of the Kingdom. Think about your own personal set of keys for moment. Most people carry at least their car keys, house keys, and often keys that pertain to their job on the same key ring. Your car key won't open your house and your house key won't start your car. Each one is designed to open or start something specific. When Jesus gives us the keys to the Kingdom, he intends for us to open or start something that is Kingdom related. That's why He gives them to us. It's not so we look good with a new set of keys, but rather so that the Kingdom of God can be expanded and advanced with words of knowledge as God gives us information about people, events, places, and other activities in the Holy Spirit that need to be revealed at a critical time.

Now, let's look a bit further into Matthew 16:21-23:

> From that time Jesus began to show to His disciples that He must go to Jerusalem, and suffer many things from the elders and chief priests and scribes, and be killed, and be raised the third day. Then Peter took Him aside and began to rebuke Him, saying, "Far be it from You, Lord; this shall not happen to You!"
>
> But He turned and said to Peter, "Get behind Me, Satan! You are an offense to Me, for you are not mindful of the things of God, but the things of men."

Jesus began to share with the disciples some of the upcoming events that would take place. He moved into a prophetic mode at this point, but Peter, the guy whose stance is named "Rock," was not too happy about it. Can you imagine that Peter began to rebuke Jesus? It was like a small pebble uploading to a large rock. Today we would say this is crazy, but Bill Johnson from Redding, California, teaches that at that time, the disciples were the most well trained people on the planet who would be carrying out the expansion of the Kingdom of God, and Peter was still in training.

But I want you to notice something. In verse seventeen, Peter is referred to one as being blessed by Jesus, and then in six short verses later in verse twenty-three, Jesus referred to Peter as the devil. First he is blessed, and then he is the devil. Notice how fast this transition happens. What is the problem? Jesus answered that question in verse twenty-three when He said that Peter was not mindful of the things of God but the things of men.

And it can happen that fast to you and to me. One moment we are totally motivated by the Kingdom of God and are hearing from the Father and downloading words of knowledge, and just a few moments later, our minds have wandered, and we are engaged with something else around us that distracts us from the presence of God. (A good illustration of this will be included in the next chapter entitled "Beep.")

One moment we are so tuned in to what God is doing, and we are moving and activating the Kingdom. Then a few minutes later, our thoughts have taken us so far away from the Kingdom that we might also be accused by Jesus for being on the devil's side.

Here's what happens when move away from the Kingdom. Above and in verse eighteen, the Word of God tells us that the gates of hell will not prevail against us. What does that mean? It means that gates are defensive weapons. As a defensive weapon, they stand there closed, keeping others out. They were never meant to be an offensive weapon such as a bodyguard with a gun who can keep people out with deadly force.

Gates were designed to be defensive weapons, and God knew that and He believed that the only way that Christians would not be effective is if they did not charge the gates. But I have to think that in this section of Scripture and others, God believed that we would indeed charge the gates of hell. He trusted that we would break them down as we endeavored to rescue countless people who felt trapped by the devil and were in demonic realms with demonic authority. Jude 1:22 says, "Some with fear, pulling them out of the fire, hating even the garment defiled by the flesh." This indicates that some are willing to crash the gates of hell to save some from the deadly fire that they are so close to entering.

If you charge the gates of hell, using the gifts of the Spirit with the authority of the Keys of the Kingdom, God promises that those gates will not remain closed, but they will give way. They will not prevail, but they will open and most likely be torn from their hinges, being flung wide open so that many can escape.

We are told in John 10:10 that the enemy comes to kill, rob, and destroy, but that Jesus has come to give us life and life abundantly. That abundant life includes being free from the ongoing attacks and destruction of the devil. How do I know this? Look at 1 John 3:8-9.

> He who sins is of the devil, for the devil has sinned from the beginning. For this purpose the Son of God was manifested, that He might destroy the works of the

devil. Whoever has been born of God does not sin, for
His seed remains in him; and he cannot sin, because he
has been born of God.

God was manifested to destroy the works of the devil and Jesus
told us that we would do the same things He did and greater.
So we also have the mandate to destroy the works of the devil,
including charging the closed gates of hell. But notice also verse
nine. The seed of almighty God remains in us. You've got to
know that whatever and whenever God plants something, it is
going to grow. That seed is Jesus and the Word of God, which
are one. When the Word is planted or grafted into our hearts,
it is not meant to be there for a short season, but for eternity.
When Jesus was baptized, the Bible says in three places that the
Holy Spirit came down and descended like a dove, but in John
1:33, we are told that the Holy Spirit remained with Jesus.

Then in Luke 3, the Spirit led Jesus into the wilderness; and in
chapter 4, the Spirit of the Lord was upon Jesus. Even in Acts
1:8, we are told that we will receive power when the Holy Spirit
comes upon us. Could it be that the power of God and the gifts
of the Holy Spirit are released in our lives when the Holy Spirit
is upon us? Let's look at Luke 4:18-19:

> The Spirit of the LORD is upon Me, because He has
> anointed Me to preach the gospel to the poor; He has
> sent Me to heal the brokenhearted, to proclaim liberty
> to the captives and recovery of sight to the blind, to
> set at liberty those who are oppressed; to proclaim the
> acceptable year of the LORD.

Could it be that when we are filled with the Holy Spirit, the fruit of the Spirit is activated from within; and when the Holy Spirit is upon us, He activates the gifts of the Spirit from the outside? I won't try to prove this thought here, but think about this. Which is more harmful to the Kingdom of God: Quenching the Holy Spirit or resisting the Holy Spirit? Resisting, deals with character and quenching deals with gifting.[2] Most would agree that both are equally important.

In John 4:5-26, we see another example of a word of knowledge, plus some additional information that will tie this all together.

> So He came to a city of Samaria which is called Sychar, near the plot of ground that Jacob gave to his son Joseph. Now Jacob's well was there. Jesus therefore, being wearied from His journey, sat thus by the well. It was about the sixth hour. A woman of Samaria came to draw water. Jesus said to her, "Give Me a drink." For His disciples had gone away into the city to buy food.
>
> Then the woman of Samaria said to Him, "How is it that You, being a Jew, ask a drink from me, a Samaritan woman?" For Jews have no dealings with Samaritans.
>
> Jesus answered and said to her, "If you knew the gift of God, and who it is who says to you, 'Give Me a drink,' you would have asked Him, and He would have given you living water."
>
> The woman said to Him, "Sir, You have nothing to draw with, and the well is deep. Where then do You get that living water? Are You greater than our father Jacob, who gave us the well, and drank from it himself, as well as his sons and his livestock?"
>
> Jesus answered and said to her, "Whoever drinks of this water will thirst again, but whoever drinks of

the water that I shall give him will never thirst. But the water that I shall give him will become in him a fountain of water springing up into everlasting life."

The woman said to Him, "Sir, give me this water, that I may not thirst, nor come here to draw."

Jesus said to her, "Go, call your husband, and come here."

The woman answered and said, "I have no husband." Jesus said to her, "You have well said, 'I have no husband,' for you have had five husbands, and the one whom you now have is not your husband; in that you spoke truly."

The woman said to Him, "Sir, I perceive that You are a prophet. Our fathers worshiped on this mountain, and you Jews say that in Jerusalem is the place where one ought to worship."

Jesus said to her, "Woman, believe Me, the hour is coming when you will neither on this mountain, nor in Jerusalem, worship the Father. You worship what you do not know; we know what we worship, for salvation is of the Jews. But the hour is coming, and now is, when the true worshipers will worship the Father in spirit and truth; for the Father is seeking such to worship Him. God is Spirit, and those who worship Him must worship in spirit and truth."

The woman said to Him, "I know that Messiah is coming" (who is called Christ). "When He comes, He will tell us all things."

Jesus said to her, "I who speak to you am He."

How many excuses do you have not to speak to people because they appear to be different from you? Perhaps they are more or less educated. Or they have more or less money. Their skin color is lighter or darker than yours. They have more or fewer body piercings and colored hair than you. Whatever your excuse is or whatever reason you are using not to talk to them, get over it. Because those excuses will indeed make the gates of hell prevail against you.

Jesus was not supposed to be talking to this Samaritan woman, and in the process, Jesus received several words of knowledge about her private dating life, and she confirmed it, recognizing that she might be in the presence of a prophet. The reality was that she had five previous husbands and was now living with still another man, and that makes six. And Jesus came on the scene. He was setting the stage very early in His ministry to teach and help people know that we are indeed the bride of Christ, and He is preparing us for that glorious wedding. While the language is not exactly pinpointed on this teaching, the Samaritan woman seemed to "get it" as she desired the fresh water that Jesus was talking about, and she also then moved out and about the city sharing with others what Jesus has done for her. Notice verses thirty-nine through forty-one:

And many of the Samaritans of that city believed in Him because of the word of the woman who testified, "He told me all that I ever did." So when the Samaritans had come to Him, they urged Him to stay with them; and He stayed there two days. And many more believed because of His own word.

This Samaritan woman also was given a word of knowledge and then given keys to begin to unlock doors that normally might have remained locked. We carry the presence of the Lord with us, and so we have the opportunity to also unlock previously locked doors.

Here is a quote by Leonard Ravenhill that I frequently share with others: "The opportunity of a lifetime must be seized within the lifetime of the opportunity."[3]

In Galatians 6:10 we read, "Therefore as you have the opportunity, do good unto all people, especially the household of faith." Find someone this week and do something good. Look for ways to bless, encourage, and manifest the Kingdom of God.

Acts 10:38 says that Jesus was anointed by the Holy Spirit and went around doing good, and yes, healing all who were oppressed by the devil too. So you have two alternatives from this verse: heal the sick, which is very possible and pretty easy; or just do good. We often miss that aspect that Jesus was anointed to do good. Surf's Up! Watch and then catch the next wave of God's Presence. There will be many opportunities if you miss the first wave or two during the week.

Chapter 1: Processing

Pray right now, asking God to reveal to you the right person to be led to, to assist, love, or be generous to. Ask God who you can pray with, give to, help, be a friend, promote, give hope, bless, share peace, buy coffee, buy a gift card, send an email, send a text, call on the phone, open a conversation about Jesus, and yes, even pray for the sick whatever He tells you. Expand the Kingdom with a Kingdom encounter!

Write down your experiences as you reach out to others. You may just be surprised to learn that what you did indeed blessed and helped others in ways that you could never have known. But God knew and told you the right person's name to bring help in a time of trouble. And by listening to the Lord for the right person to touch, you may have just received a heavenly download in the form of a word of knowledge for someone in particular. And in doing so, you may even have snatched them from the fire, because the gates of hell will not prevail against you, unless of course you do nothing.

Chapter 2

Beep

One cold and snowy January morning, I answered the phone and heard the voice of a pastor friend in the area. He is the pastor of one of the largest churches in the city, and he began to tell me about a man in his congregation who was in the hospital at that time. This man was in a coma in the intensive care unit of a hospital way on the other side of town. The pastor asked me if I would be willing to go up and pray for this man.

My initial response in my head was: *Pastor, you are the leader of one of the largest churches in town with thousands attending. Plus, you have a very large staff that could go and pray, not to mention a larger group of volunteers who have been trained in this type of healing prayer. On top of that, it is cold and snowy, and this hospital is a very long distance from my house.* But out of my mouth I heard myself say, "Of course Pastor, I will be happy to go and pray."

Later in the day, I made my way up to the hospital, and after meeting several of the man's family members, I went into the intensive care unit with his wife and his brother. Upon entering, I saw the man lying on the bed, completely unconscious, with tubes down his throat and nose. Beside his bed was a monitor that recorded his vital signs and statistics. I was told that his blood pressure was very high and his heart rate was very low. Every two to three seconds, the monitor would beep, and a small light would blink simultaneously. There was this constant *BEEP, BEEP, BEEP,* sound in an otherwise very quiet room.

So here I was with this man in a coma, his closest family members in the room, and the monitor going *BEEP, BEEP, BEEP.* And I began to pray.

When I pray for the sick, I normally begin by calmly and quietly, yet firmly speaking healing. I proceed by asking for help from the Holy Spirit, giving glory and honor to God, and quoting Bible passages as I remember them. When I pray for someone who can answer, I will stop periodically (as directed by the Holy Spirit) to inquire as to how this person may be feeling. But, of course, this man could not answer.

My guess is that I was praying for about ten minutes, when suddenly the *BEEP* of the monitor caught my attention. I began to read the stats on the monitor, and I noticed that his heart rate was decreasing even further and his blood pressure was increasing. Both of these stats happening simultaneously was not a good sign. I began to worry and think to myself: *Oh no! This guy is going to die. This is going to look real good on my resume. I can see it now: Pastor of largest church in town calls and asks me to pray, and the patient dies while I am praying for him.*

Please understand, I had not stopped praying for this man. The other two people in the room had no idea that I was watching the monitor and having these thoughts, because I just kept right on speaking healing and praying as I had been doing prior to this.

And then God began to speak to me. He began by reminding me that we walk by faith and not by sight, and that it was necessary and important to stop watching the monitor. He also reminded me that I had a calling to pray for the sick and that He was in control of the situation in that room. So at this point, I was still praying, but I was watching the monitor and listening to the repeated *BEEP* sound. Meanwhile, I was having doubtful thoughts while simultaneously listening to God speak to me. I was multi-tasking *BIG* time.

After a short while, I was able to get back on track and keep praying for this man, even though the vital signs actually were getting worse. I will be honest and share that it took a bit of time for me to refocus and get on the right course, but God was gracious and helped me in the process.

After I felt released from the prayer time, the man's family and I went out in the hallway and shared individual cell numbers with each other. I shared that I would be happy to return and pray again at a later date if that was something that they wanted me to do.

The next day, I received a phone call from the man's wife, and she asked me if I could return. I noticed that her voice sounded different, so I asked her what was going on. She responded by informing me that her husband had awakened and that he wanted to meet me!

I was not able to get up to the hospital that day, but I went the next day and found the man awake in his own private room. After I met the man, his doctor entered and told me that he had never seen anyone in a coma in that condition wake up that fast. That was a blessing, and of course God is amazing and gets all of the credit and glory for this wonderful healing.

But I have often wondered what might have happened if I had continued to watch the monitor. What would have happened if I had not been able to get back on track? Thankfully, God, in His great compassion for that man and his family, spoke to me in the middle of my doubt and unbelief and still performed a great miracle that was a blessing to many. Another download from heaven occurred.

In 3 John 3-4, we read these words: "For I rejoiced greatly when brethren came and testified of the truth that is in you, just as you walk in the truth. I have no greater joy than to hear that my children walk in truth." This is a tremendous Scripture with a great proclamation of sincerity and honesty. Nothing is of greater joy to God than to hear of His children walking in truth. Since Jesus is the Way, the Truth, and the Life (according to John 14:6), it would seem critical that we hear the truth in every area of our lives. And Jesus is so faithful to share that truth that He will interrupt our prayers to get us back on track with simple yet firm commands like, "Stop watching the monitor."

For you see, the monitor and the *BEEP, BEEP, BEEP*, are symptoms of two major hindrances to our walk with God and our prayer life: attractions and distractions. Each of us has both of those obstacles that interfere with our ability to flow with the Holy Spirit and to be responsive to the voice of the Lord. Henry

Ford once said, "Obstacles are those frightful things you see when you take your eyes off your goal."[4]

The goal at the hospital was to help this man avoid future medical obstacles and get off the ventilator. However, the obstacles that I saw greatly reduced my ability to walk by faith. Instead, I was distracted by the *BEEP, BEEP, BEEP,* which in turn directed my focus away from trusting God and into the realm of the visible. But God is the God of the invisible and the unseen realm. Hebrews 11:1 says, "Now faith is the substance of things hoped for, the evidence of things not seen." My good friend Dr. Neil Kanning (who wrote one of the recommendations for this book) states that faith should be spelled R-I-S-K, because we are almost always making decisions and acting based on information from God about things that we can't see.

The more we listen and respond to God, the greater the risk. Scripture tells us that we go from glory to glory,[5] strength to strength,[6] and faith to faith.[7] It's those times and seasons of faith that will develop the character and inner strength to help us in the future when we need it most. It is important for us to remain faithful now and walk in Biblical truth. Then we can avoid *BEEPING* obstacles that distract us from having a closer walk with Jesus.

Chapter 2: Processing

Can you think of a time when you had an opportunity to do something for the Lord, but there was an obstacle that prevented you from fulfilling His plan? Did you learn anything from that experience that would help you avoid the same conclusion or outcome in the future? Would you be willing to stop right now and set three attainable goals to help you prevent this from happening in the future? Perhaps you could write them in a journal or even at the bottom of this page. After you list the goals, pray to God and ask Him to help you keep these goals and to give you the strength to grow to a place where the *beeps* in your life are not such major distractions.

Chapter 3

Armpit

When I was forty-nine, a friend of mine invited me to lead a chapel service at a local Christian high school. I have to admit, I was pretty apprehensive. At my age, what could I say or share that would relate to a room full of teenagers? But I accepted the invitation because I like new challenges and because the person who invited me felt I could contribute to a positive spiritual climate in that school.

I was told in advance that the students would be polite and listen, but they would not respond to any offer for prayer. My talk was on power encounters with God. I purposed in my heart to deliver a message that would be relevant to the students, hopefully drawing them into the Kingdom of God.

When I arrived, I encountered one hundred students packed into a small room. The service began with some contemporary praise and worship led by a student worship band. After that, a PowerPoint video with excerpts from the *Chronicles of Narnia* movie was shown on the screen. At the conclusion of the video, I got up and stated, "That was Hollywood, but now let me tell you about the power of God." For the next fifteen minutes I shared and afterward gave the students an opportunity to come forward for prayer to get right with God. Amazingly enough, forty-five of the one hundred students came forward, experiencing individual and group prayer ministry, as well as words of knowledge spoken over them. These students stayed for another hour, missing their next class. Keep in mind, I was told that they would not respond to any offer for ministry.

After the chapel service, the principal of the school approached me and told me that it appeared that God was doing something special for the students and the school. He then asked me if I could return the following Monday afternoon. The school does not normally have a chapel service at that time, but he wanted the student body to experience more of God. The time slot selected was the last hour of the school day, so that if any of the students wanted prayer, they could stay after school on their own time and not miss classes. (Some of the faculty had a tough time with partial to half-full classes during the previous chapel.) The principal also told me that the junior high would be joining the high school for the chapel, thus bringing the student population to one hundred sixty for the service. Of course, I agreed to return.

After the praise and worship time, a strange thing happened. Many of the staff got up and shared lengthy announcements. When I got up to speak, I literally had only seven minutes left before the final bell was supposed to ring. To this day, I have no idea what I talked about, but after my short message, one hundred twenty students stood for prayer. I offered individual prayer ministry with these students on their own time until 5:15 p.m. Just like the first chapel, I was blessed with many words of knowledge that led many of the students to weep and repent, breaking into spontaneous prayer groups and lingering with Jesus.

Before sharing what happened at the third chapel, I need to rewind and backtrack a bit and share another story that happened four months prior to my invitation to lead the chapel.

I was invited to lead a healing service at a large Lutheran church here in Omaha. In preparation for the service, God spoke to me at home and told me that a lady would be healed of a wheezing cough during the service. I asked the Lord if this was due to a cold or the flu, and He said, "No, it is Mendelson's Disease." I am not a doctor, so I had no idea what Mendelson's Disease was. Upon completing an Internet search, I discovered that Mendelson's Disease is "a...condition in which acid fluid from the stomach is brought up into the windpipe and passes into the lungs."[8] These fluids would get lodged in her throat, causing her to cough.

God also spoke to me and said there would be a man attending who had a cyst in his right armpit, and that he had never asked for prayer because he was embarrassed by the cyst's location. At the conclusion of my message, I shared the information about the cough, and two ladies responded. One stated that her doctor had just informed her that, while it was rare, it might be Mendelson's Disease. Later, I learned that her chronic cough was completely healed in a very short amount of time.

At this point I was feeling pretty confident, so I shared with the congregation about the man with the cyst in the armpit. But no one responded. I did not let the silence in the room cause a *BEEP* to go off, so I shared the word again. Finally, from the back of the room, a man raised his hand, sheepishly admitting that he was the one, and that he had never asked for prayer because he was indeed embarrassed by the location. He came forward for prayer, and all of the pain associated with that cyst disappeared.

What I did not know at the time was that this man, along with several others and their pastor, were there in the service to observe me. They wanted to see if I was credible and authentic to come to their Mennonite Brethren church to teach and minister. As a result, they invited me to minister there four months later.

In the morning service at that church, many people responded for prayer. The altar area was so packed that I had to stay at the front and point at people while sharing what I was hearing from the Lord regarding their circumstances. This ministry propelled us into the evening service when I taught on the fire and anointing of God. Again, the place was packed with hungry people.

At the conclusion of the message, and as I was about to pray for people, I noticed a young teenager lingering towards the front. It appeared to me that the anointing of the Lord was all over her, so I approached her and asked if she would like to pray for people in the room. She shared that she had never done that, but I assured her that I would be near and could coach her as needed. I also stated that I thought we should ask the pastor if it was okay. After talking with him briefly, he assured me it would be okay. This girl, who was fifteen years old at the time, began to pray very passionate prayers of faith over many people. Sometimes she had direct words of knowledge, and other times she spoke prophetically, often weeping and crying over those for whom she was praying.

I was later introduced to her and learned that she was the pastor's daughter. But God had not revealed that to me at the time. Psalm 119:105 says that the Word of God is a lamp unto my feet, and a light unto my path. The picture here is simple and twofold: The lamp unto my feet is like a living room lamp that gives just enough light to read a book or a magazine, but the light unto the path is like the backyard spotlight that lights up the whole yard. Sometimes the Lord gives just enough light for the immediate revelation, and other times He gives substantially more information. My point is that if God had told me that this girl was the pastor's daughter, I most likely would not have approached him and asked her to pray, since I would not have wanted to put him in a potentially difficult position within his denomination.

Now, let's fast-forward to my third chapel service at the Christian high school. Because this girl was in home school at the time, I invited her and her dad to come with me. After sharing briefly with the one hundred sixty students, I then invited her to come forward and share her testimony from the previous Sunday evening. She talked for nearly fifteen minutes about getting hot for God, listening to His voice, and responding even when it is extremely uncomfortable to do so. When she was finished, the student body gave her a lengthy standing ovation. Let me tell you, youth and students just don't normally respond that way. We then had another extended time of prayer ministry, with many of the students coming to both this girl and me for prayer. And this all opened up because of a unique word from the Lord about a man with an armpit problem.

Armpits aren't the best, are they? We may forget to brush our teeth, or use cologne or perfume, but we rarely forget our deodorant. Why? Because body odor is offensive. In Isaiah 3:24, God says regarding the wicked, that instead of a sweet aroma, there will be a stench. The word *wicked* means "twisted," and we get other words such as *candlewick* and *wicker* furniture from the same root word.[9] The point is that when we allow twisted thinking to take us away from trusting God, and when we rely more on either what we can see or what we have previously experienced, we potentially set up a scenario where we stink, spiritually speaking. At best, we have armpit mentality that needs refreshing. Remember, Ecclesiastes 10:1 says, "Dead flies putrefy the perfumer's ointment, and cause it to give off a foul odor; so does a little folly to one respected for wisdom and honor."

God used an armpit to open up doors of ministry for me to go to the Mennonite Brethren church, and for this home schooled girl to go to the Christian high school to share. There are many more testimonies that came as a result of her sharing—too numerous to write here. But let me assure you that God knew what He was doing, and through His revealed Word, great ministry opportunities continue to happen. Even now as you are reading this testimony, I just have to believe that the Lord is stimulating something in you. I believe He is causing you to step out with renewed and energized faith so you can anticipate making a difference in the life of someone you know.

Chapter 3: Processing

Can you recall a time when God either spoke to you and it did not make sense to you, or He asked you to do something that seemed crazy to you? Psalm 37:23 says that the steps of righteous people are ordered by the Lord. What direction are you facing right now? Which way is the Lord leading? I am intentionally not asking you to remember how you responded in the past, but rather asking you to spend some time with God right now, seeking Him for how He wants to use you today, this week, or this month.

The Kingdom of God is always in front of you, not behind you. Luke 9:62 verifies this, stating, "No one, having put his hand to the plow, and looking back, is fit for the kingdom of God." Please pause right now and ask the Lord to begin taking you on a path that will implement the Kingdom of God in your life and the lives of others too. Listen to what He tells you, and write down what you hear.

Chapter 4

$20

Remember the chapel services I was invited to lead at the local Christian junior/senior high school in town? I talked about them in the previous chapter entitled "Armpit." But now, I want to go into more detail about specific stories from a couple of those chapel services. The second chapel service at the school was the one where I had seven minutes to talk, and one hundred twenty students stayed after school until 5:15 p.m. for prayer ministry. The prayers were sincere and on target, again with many words of knowledge. God would download information about each student to me that was previously only known by that student and maybe his/her close friends. It certainly was not public information. God revealed interesting facts ranging from specific problems at home or at school, to what kind of car they wanted or how many brothers and sisters they had—even their favorite color.

I will never forget when one particular young lady student with blonde hair came forward. She was genuinely excited to discover how and what God might speak to her. As I started to pray over her, I heard the Lord say, "Tell her that I like purple." So that is exactly what I told her.

She had a funny, yet inquisitive look on her face, so I asked her if she liked purple. She nodded her head. When I asked if it was her favorite color, she readily replied that it was. I proceeded by asking if she was kind of elaborate about it, and if her friends teased her because of her excessive use of that color. She said that they got on her about it all the time.

So I just said, "Well, God wanted you to know that He created the color purple and that He really likes it." She just beamed and began to tell everyone in the room how God likes purple.

I was invited back a short time later for still another chapel, and this time, in the middle of my message, God instructed me to go up to a certain girl and give her $20. So I stopped talking to the larger group, walked up to this young lady, pulled a $20 bill out of my wallet, and offered it to her. She asked what I was doing, and I told her that God told me to give her $20.

Her eyes began to puddle and mist. I inquired as to what was happening, and she responded by stating that she did not believe in God and that her parents made her go to this school. She said she really did not understand this revival that was going on in the school, but that very morning she had prayed and just asked God this question: "Hey, God, if You are real, have someone give me $20 today."

Later, during the prayer ministry time, she came forward and surrendered her life to the Lord. Her friends then came up to me and declared that they were amazed, because if there was one student in the school that they thought would never get right with God, it was this girl. They went on to tell me that she often got into trouble and was into all sorts of deviant behavior. She was into Wicca and also cutting, which is why she frequently wore long sleeves to school.

I later thought, *Wow! What a way for God to grab someone's attention. It only cost me $20, but it cost Jesus His life. Yes, He was willing to die for her too.*

Since this may be the only chapter that I talk about finances, I would like to share a bit about something I call, "This is not my recession." As this book is being written, America and many other nations are experiencing a tough financial recession that is affecting many people who have lost their jobs, their pensions, their homes, and their usual livelihood. In these next paragraphs, I do not mean to minimize their situation at all. But I also want to help you who are reading this book to grab a Kingdom perspective.

The word perspective means the science of optics, relating to vision and seeing. We actually get two words from the word *perspective*. The first is *outlook*, which is a way of thinking or a point of view. The second is *lookout*, which means to be carefully watching for something with anticipation.

So *outlook* is a way of thinking and *lookout* is the actual viewing coupled with thinking. In the movie *Facing the Giants* the coach takes a chance on a young new field goal kicker, and when challenged by the other coaches on staff, he responds, "I'm preparing for rain."[10] That's a great picture of outlook and lookout combined into a life changing perspective. So let's see if we can apply that toward the current recession or any other economic problems you may be facing as you read this book.

Let's analyze the word *recession*. *Re* is a prefix, and it means to go back. Most words with the prefix *re* mean to go back to something (i.e. reschedule, restore, retell, etc.). And the word *cession* means to surrender. So in a recession, it is easy for people to want to go back and surrender to an old way, an old habit, or an old standard that is usually worldly in nature and without any Kingdom benefits.

But we are supposed to be Kingdom people. Jesus told us in the Bible to preach the Kingdom wherever we go. He told us to seek first the Kingdom (Matt. 6:33). Over and over in the Gospels, we read and hear a lot about the Kingdom of God. We even pray in what many call the Lord's Prayer, "Thy Kingdom come . . . on earth as it [already] is in heaven" (Matt. 6:10). So we must ask these questions: Is there a recession in heaven? Are there foreclosures in heaven for the mansions of those who have already gone ahead of us? Is there sickness or depression in heaven? Of course, the answer to these questions is an obvious "no" in each case.

We should therefore start believing that God wants to manifest His Kingdom from heaven on earth. In essence, the Lord wants to franchise the Kingdom of God right here on earth, in the town that you live, the church you attend, and the business you work for, with your family, friends, and neighbors. The word *manifest* means to be brought to the light, to be made known, to be revealed, and to become conspicuous. The reason that so many believers do not experience more Kingdom manifestations with these definitions is that they have become disenfranchised from the Kingdom.

This happens for many reasons, but the bottom line is most believers just don't want to respond to the Lord as He would have them respond. You see, if you decide to open a franchise—whether that be McDonalds, GNC, Starbucks, or Holiday Inn—you must do it with the same standards and same model as the parent company.

Let's just examine McDonalds for a moment. Let's pretend that you want to open a new McDonalds in your town, and you get permission from the corporation to proceed. They give you strict guidelines—including color schemes, signage, health care benefits, menu items, and so on—and you are working towards your grand opening. But McDonalds seems to have some menu items missing that other fast food restaurants have, like tacos. Since you have been to Taco Bell and enjoyed one of its taco combinations that includes tomatoes and sour cream, you decide to add that one item to your menu. One week before your grand opening, the district manager for McDonalds comes in for his last inspection, and your signage is correct, your colors are right on, and your health care plan is in order. But while he is looking at your menu board, suddenly he blurts out, "What are those tacos doing on the menu?!"

You tell the district manager how much you like these tacos at Taco Bell and how many people buy them, and that you thought this would make a great new addition to the menu at your new McDonalds, but the manager exclaims, "That taco item is not on the McDonalds national menu, and is not a part of the franchise! You must remove it, or you can't open your new McDonalds!" You are shocked because you have spent months, perhaps a year or two, working toward this big event. Even though you feel like you know what is best for McDonalds based on your experience with these tacos, if you don't do it the way McDonalds asks you to, you can't open the franchise.

What happened? There was a *beep*. There was a taco attraction. As a result, you became disenfranchised along the way, so you are now faced with a choice to make. You can open up something that kind of looks like McDonalds but is not the real deal, or you can remove the tacos from the menu, follow the guidelines, and open up the McDonalds like the parent company told you to do.

The same principle applies with God and his Word. He has given us commands and procedures from the Bible for us to follow, but we often think we have a better idea. We use excuses like, "We need to be culturally relevant," or "God will understand," or even, "God told me it is okay." Yet, it contradicts what is in the Word of God. Many go off on their own, but they don't really succeed. They don't really prosper. What they get is something that is only half correct, but had they gone all the way with God and done it the way He told them to, they would have really been blessed.

I like this definition used in Chapter 1 of the word *blessed*: To prosper and be in control of every situation, regardless. It really comes down to simple obedience. I don't have time to teach and share the whole message called "This Is Not My Recession" here in this book, but I would encourage you to begin to change your perspective. Change your viewpoint. Change your outlook and lookout.

We are Kingdom people, and according to Acts 17:28, it is in Jesus that we live and move and have our being. So while we do look at the stock market, we aren't moved by it because we move in the Lord. And while we may study the real estate market, we don't live there. Of course it is okay for us to keep track of our investments, but we must make sure that our Kingdom investments are cared for as well. We need to move away from fear and worry that so often accompanies the world's way of doing things, and instead begin to trust God in every financial situation.

As for me and my family, we have given away furniture, appliances, food, clothes, small sums of money, larger sums of money, cars, and even land. In every case, God worked it all out so incredibly well. We never missed a beat financially, and we were always blessed back in what we gave away, because the Bible clearly states that whatever a person shall sow, he shall reap. I am not talking about prosperity hype, but rather just basic Kingdom principles that set us up to prosper and to be ready to give at a moment's notice when He asks us to bless someone.

I wonder what would have happened if I had chosen not to give the $20 away, but instead had just asked if anyone in the room could use $20. Probably every hand would have gone up, and I could have weaved that question into the message. But God knew that a particular young lady who was so against Him actually prayed a prayer that morning that if God was real, would He have someone give her $20 that day.

There is no recession in heaven, so I am just agreeing with the Bible when it says to pray, "Thy Kingdom come, Thy will be done, on earth, as it is in heaven." I gave you the definition of recession above, but I did not share what God wants us to do or where God wants to take us. I believe he wants us to move from *recession* and go to *inter*cession. *Re* means to go back, so recession has some aspect of going back to it. But advancing the Kingdom is about going forward. As I quoted in the last chapter, Jesus said in Luke 9:62, "No one having put his hand to the plow and looking back is fit for the Kingdom of God." When Jesus uses the words *no one*, He is including everyone. No exceptions.

Now we often think of intercession as being prayer, and it definitely has that meaning. But *inter* means to go into, and *cession* still means to surrender. So instead of a recession which is based on the past, God wants us to move from the past and recession to intercession, which deals with the future. God would like us to go forward and surrender to His ways. To go deeper into the Kingdom and trust Him when he says, "Add another zero to that check. Give your furniture away. Bless someone behind you in the drive-thru at Starbucks. Pay for someone's groceries. Give $20 away to someone at church." These are the ways and means that God uses to discover if you are ready for promotion. If you are faithful in the small things, and the insignificant things, He will then make you a ruler over cities and bless you mightily (see Luke 19:17-19). But the requirement of stewards is faithfulness, according to 2 Corinthians 4:2, and we are stewards of everything God has given us.

What kind of steward will you be? Will you stay connected to the Kingdom franchise, or will you eventually become disenfranchised? Are you willing to take on the Kingdom attitude and move forward, or will you be content to continue to look in the past, and then someday when you are old, wonder why you never got to the destination that God had for you? Will you trust God now or will you continue to operate with the same old broken-down system that never seems to get you anywhere? It is your choice. God is not a respecter of people, but He is a respecter of choices. He clearly states in the Bible that He has set life and death in front of you, and you can choose (Deut. 30:19). He gives us the option in our choices. And then He honors those choices.

If we choose something less than the Kingdom, He does not force it on us, but allows us to walk out our choices. But if we choose His ways, His thoughts, and His processes, then we get to really experience the abundant life that Jesus proclaimed in John 10. But of course, it is your choice. So my challenge to you today is: Don't go back to a recession. Go forward to intercession. Yes, it means prayer, but it also means to go into the Kingdom, to stay connected to the franchise, and not to become disenfranchised. Be faithful with what the Lord has given you and what He tells you to do with what He has given you.

Chapter 4: Processing

Do you remember a time when God asked you to give something to someone without asking for anything in return? Do you recall a time when God spoke to you and interrupted your schedule, asking you to respond in a way that was out of the ordinary or inconvenient? What was your response? How did you process this? Did it scare you or make you nervous to hear God in this way?

Isaiah 1:19 says that if we are willing and obedient, God will give us the good of the land. Many believers are willing, but few reach the obedient stage. Others are obedient but respond in an unwilling way, only because they are forced to. It may not involve giving money away, although it could. But it might be a really simple task such as sending an email or text message of encouragement, or calling someone on the phone to check on him and offering to pray with him. It might include buying a gift card for somebody or taking that person out for coffee. But whatever the assignment, try to remember that God does these things for a reason, using people like us to advance His Kingdom.

Take time to pray right now and ask God to help you be willing and obedient at a moment's notice. Ask Him to help you have a Kingdom mindset that will always respond favorably and quickly. You don't want to miss the opportunity that God may have for you and for the person that needs your touch, your prayer, and your helpfulness. You may remember learning in Chapter 1 on *Teaching* that Leonard Ravenhill said, "The opportunity of a lifetime must be seized within the lifetime of the opportunity." Seize your opportunity today!

Chapter 5

Waiting

Here in the Omaha area I have been honored and privileged to minister at over 100 churches, schools, and businesses in a variety of ways. One of those churches is a smaller African American Church where the pastor and I have shared mutual friendship and a similar Kingdom understanding for many years.

Whenever we would attend there, we had to sit on very hard and narrow pews. One day I simply asked him if they had ever thought about getting chairs to replace the pews, and he responded that they had thought about it many times and had even priced some chairs. I asked him what the price was, and he told me that the ones they wanted would cost $5500 for one hundred chairs. Now that is a lot of money for a small church of around sixty people.

I decided to pray about how we could help him get his chairs, and I came up with a plan that my wife Diane and I thought we could manage. That plan was that we would give $1000 toward the chairs and then ask other churches in the community to help with the remaining $4500 of donations. But when praying, I then felt led to ask only one local church, and it was one of the largest churches in Omaha.

So our plan was set, but I felt like I needed to ask God for the right timing. Every time I approached God about this option to ask the senior pastor of this large church, I felt like God was saying to wait. Now, this went on for several months. In the meantime, the pastor of the church that needed the chairs would occasionally come to me and inquire about the status of the chairs, and I would have to simply respond that God had me in a holding pattern to ask for the additional funds.

This literally went on for eight months, and then one day, I felt a release to approach the senior pastor of this large church. I sent him a letter outlining my plan and request, and soon after that I received a quick reply, with a positive answer that they would indeed help and provide the additional $4500.

But here is the kicker. That pastor told me that if I had come to him a few days earlier or a week earlier or a month earlier he would have turned me down. He went on to say that in the previous days and months, they just did not have any extra to share, but they owned some land that they hoped to expand on someday. The state of Nebraska had come in and purchased some of that land for a road expansion, and the state gave their church a substantial amount of money. The elders of the church had just decided specifically to tithe off of that increase and give it into ministry in the city, and I was the first person to come and ask for funds just after that decision had been made.

I know that if I had ignored God's voice to wait and had asked sooner, that pastor would have turned me down, and I would never have gone back to him later and asked again. So God specifically knew the timing and gave me the words of knowledge to wait. By waiting, I was able to help this other church, and they received their new chairs and have them to this day.

Psalm 27:14 says, "Wait on the Lord, be of good courage, and He shall strengthen your heart. Wait I say on the Lord." Psalm 40:1 goes like this: "When I waited patiently for the Lord, he inclined to me and heard my cry." The word *inclined* means he leaned over to talk to me. I like that. There is something so cool about knowing that God is so interested in us that he would lean over to share with us. I hope you agree.

We live in a society that says, "Hurry up and wait." We wait at the doctor or the dentist, and we wait for dial-ups, upgrades and downloads. We wait at the grocery store, hardware store and department store. We wait in slow moving lines at fast food restaurants. We wait in traffic while driving to a nice restaurant. We may wait in line to eat at the nice restaurant, wait to order at the same restaurant, wait for the food to arrive, and then wait in more traffic driving home.

We wait at airports to check in, to go through security, and to wait at the gate. Then we wait to get on the plane and wait while others get on the plane, only to have the flight attendants try to hurry us along. Once we are finally seated, the flight attendants tell us that there is a delay that causes us to wait longer. The plane finally begins to back up only to find us waiting more on the runway to take off. We wait while we fly to our destination and finally get close to landing, only to hear the pilot tell us that we will be circling for a while. Then we finally land but have to wait for the jet bridge to be moved over to the plane so the door can be opened. We then wait to get off, wait for our luggage, and wait at the rental car counter or to get a shuttle to our hotel, where we wait in more lines to register and get checked in. Wait, I think I missed something.

We wait for our car to be repaired and for a prescription to be filled. We wait in line at the movies to get in and then at the concession stand. We wait at sporting events and in bathroom lines. We wait in church during the offering for some unprepared person to write a check, or for the pastor to finish his sermon. And someone reading this right now is waiting for me to get done with this exhortation on waiting. And we wait, and we wait, and we wait, but we don't want to wait on God.

Look at these excerpts from various Psalms in the Bible:

- 31:2: Deliver me speedily.
- 69:17: Hear Me speedily.
- 102:2: Answer me quickly.
- 38:22: Make Haste to help me.
- 70:1: Make haste to deliver me.
- 141:1: Lord, I cry out to you. Make haste unto me. Give ear unto my voice when I pray.

And I would ask: Why should He? It seems like we are constantly asking God to hurry up and catch up with us and our problems and our difficulties, with words like Help Me Now. And God says, "Wait."

We don't like that word.

But God is an investor, and He enjoys investing time into our lives because he has eternal purposes planned for our lives. The time we now spend learning and growing will aid us and assist us in the future, so we need to learn to trust God when He asks us to wait. To be honest, it was not pleasant to wait all of those months to ask that one pastor for that $4500 while I had to keep sharing with the other pastor why I did not have the money yet for his chairs. Have you been there? Where you were waiting on God or even someone else for an extended period of time, but felt foolish in the process? I think God does this from time to time just to see if we really will trust in Him, regardless.

This waiting process also helps to build patience in us. James 1:14 reads, "Let patience have her perfect work that you may be perfect and complete, lacking nothing." God wants our trust, and waiting often perfects us in many realms so that when He does call on us for an immediate response, we are complete, lacking nothing, and ready to respond.

Dr. Richard Moss says that the greatest gift you can give another is the purity of your attention. In the Bible, the word *Selah* appears seventy-seven times, most of those in the Psalms, but also in Habakkuk. And the word *Selah* means to pause and rest. It represents a rest like in music, which often designates a change or a new sense of direction. *Selah* often leads to active ministry which cannot be envisioned without a *Selah* time, to pause, think, and reflect while quietly waiting.

Psalm 46:10 instructs us to be still and know that God is God. The people in the American contemporary church do not like to be still. For some reason it bothers them. The contemporary Christians in America like movement, noise, and activity. They like to be busy. Keep in mind that God did not rest because He was tired, but rather he rested because He was finished.[11] So while God does call us to finish strong, He does not call us to be busy all of the time. And sometimes, we actually need the season of rest before starting that new task.

I believe it is Rick Joyner whose ministry takes a break every August. They just close the doors to the church and encourage people to take a month off to rest. They also encourage them to visit other churches in the area. I think this is a great plan. I know that years ago while I was serving as a pastor in Kansas, we would take a whole week off periodically just to take a rest week. No services, no meetings, no gatherings, and yes, that meant no offerings at the services we missed. But God is our source and provider, and we never had a problem.

First Thessalonians 4:11 asks us to aspire to lead a quiet life. The King James Version says, "Study to be quiet." Is it really that difficult for us that we need to study the concept of being quiet? *Selah* again means to study to be quiet, and it is an activity of not having an activity. We are just to pause and become mindful of the presence of the Lord, and enjoy that presence without working it up, hyping it up, or producing something. Just be still, and know that He is God.

Isaiah 30:15-16 gives this advice: "In returning and rest you shall be saved. In quietness and confidence shall be your strength, but you would not. And you said, 'No, for we will flee on horses.' Therefore you shall flee, and we will ride on swift horses." Let's modernize it a bit. We will keep busy and watch many movies and sporting events. We will invest in the stock market and real estate and then fret over how those investments are doing, spending much time analyzing them. And we will keep busy with iPods, iPads, computers, texting, email, Facebook, and whatever electronic means we have. This includes CDs, DVDs, and Blu-Ray. Our pace will pick up to a frenzy as we add in more and more activities, events, and gatherings with our friends, at work, with our neighbors, and at church—oh, for sure at church! Let's get really busy and work and work and work, but not bear fruit, because bearing fruit just takes too long, and I don't have time to wait.

Isaiah 30:18 imparts to us, "Blessed are those who wait." But I thought I was blessed if I am busy. God says you are blessed when you wait. There are seasons to wait. Say it out loud: "I am blessed when I wait." Say it again. Say it slowly.

Lamentations 3:24-25 instructs us with these words – "The Lord is my portion, therefore I hope in Him. The Lord is good to those who wait for Him." Our society constantly says, "Hurry up and wait." God says that He is good to those who wait for Him. In Luke 2:25 we learn that "Simeon was righteous, devout and waiting and that the Holy Spirit was upon him." Did you catch that? I thought the Holy Spirit was on people who were busy and active and rapidly going after something. Not always. There is peace and a calming effect that brings the Holy Spirit on some-one who genuinely is waiting for God. This kind of person loves to wait for God and is not in a hurry, but delights in doing what God asks, including waiting, if that is what He wants.

So the word of the Lord in this chapter might be S-L-O-W—D-O-W-N. And I conclude with Psalm 27:4: "Wait on the Lord, be of good courage, and He will strengthen your heart."

One more time, say out loud, "I am blessed when I wait." Now, do it.

Chapter 5: Processing

- Stop.
- Wait.
- Listen.
- Selah.
- Repeat.

Chapter 6

Watch

B ack in the mid-1990's, I was a pastor in rural Kansas. Previous to that, I had been on staff at a Spirit-filled Lutheran Church in Texas, but I felt led to accept an offer to go to this small rural church in a small rural town out in the plains of Kansas. Overall, it was a great experience and I learned a lot. One of the things I learned was to depend on God even more than when we were in the suburbs where we had a Wal-Mart, a Walgreens, many great restaurants, and so on the list goes. When we moved to this town, there were two banks, two motels, a Pizza Hut, and a couple of home-grown restaurants.

When we arrived, we began to pray that the town would prosper, and four years later we had three banks, four hotels, and more restaurants, including a McDonalds. But it was not a very large McDonalds. I would often kid and say you could not get a Big Mac there, but only a Little Mac.

Anyway, that leads me to this next story. One summer, as a congregation, we decided to go to a conference in Kansas City, only about an eight-hour drive across the state of Kansas. I knew that some of the folks from our church attending the conference would want to do some shopping, so we budgeted time in expressly for that to happen.

One of the things I wanted to purchase was a watch. Now, we had a fairly nice pharmacy in our little rural town, and they had a variety of Timex watches, but I really wanted something a bit different. In fact, I had my specifications all laid out. I had prayed about it and spent time discussing possible costs with my wife too.

I wanted a watch with a black wristband, a white face with gold hands and a second hand, and for the watch to have Roman numerals, a day and date calendar, plus something that would be shock resistant. I wanted it to be a little nicer than a Timex, and my wife and I had agreed that it would be okay for me to have a nice watch to wear, especially for church and more formal functions. There are not many formal functions in a rural town, but you never know!

Anyway, at one point on our Saturday afternoon in Kansas City, there was an extended break, so we all went to a mall because, like I said, many wanted to go shopping. I headed off to look for my watch and soon came to a store that had watches in the display case. I went inside, and guess what I found? The exact watch with the exact specifications that I wanted—and it was $150.00. Now that did seem a bit extravagant even for me, but my wife and I had set a ceiling of what I could spend, and that was within the limit. So after trying it on, I started to get my credit card out to pay for it, but God spoke to me and said, "If you wait, you will find it cheaper tomorrow."

Well, tomorrow was Sunday, and right after the final morning service, we were all going to head back home on our eight-hour drive, so I argued with the Lord, telling Him what I knew and obviously what He did not know. This sounds like the example of Peter rebuking Jesus in the chapter called "Teaching." But when I was done speaking to the Lord, He simply stated again, "If you wait, you will find it cheaper tomorrow." This was a big dilemma for me because I knew our schedule and I knew how far we lived from the city. I really was not too keen on taking a chance. Yet, I also knew what the voice of the Lord sounded like, and this really did sound like Him. So, I decided not to buy the watch, even though I really did want that watch. It was a tough decision.

On Sunday, we went to church and we met some folks who wanted to have lunch with us, and as a group we decided we wanted to connect with these folks who happened to live in Kansas City. We suggested that they select a restaurant for us to eat at. And wouldn't you know it; they picked a restaurant that was in a mall. When we arrived at the restaurant, we found out that there was a forty-five minute wait. During the wait, some decided to go shopping again, and I was one of them.

But a mall is a big place, so I quickly repented to God and asked him to tell me where to go. If He was not so loving, I am sure He could have told me some places to go for sure, but He simply stated that I should go to J. C. Penney's.

I found the store locator on one of those large maps and headed off to Penney's, only to discover when I found the location of the watches that the entire case was empty. I was blown away and, quickly finding a sales person, I asked where all of the watches were, thinking that they had moved them to another part of the store.

The clerk knew right away what had happened and she informed me that they just completed a huge watch sale, and that they literally had sold out. I then shared my plight with her about coming from the small town eight hours away, and that I had prayed and felt like God told me there was a watch for me in that store. She listened politely and said she would go in the back and check but was doubtful that she would find anything.

She was gone for a very long time and finally emerged, carrying a watch box with one men's watch in it. I opened the box and discovered that every specification that I wanted was included. It was the exact watch that I wanted and had prayed about in advance.

I looked at her and told her the rest of the story, and she responded that this was the very last watch, and for some reason it had not sold. She insisted that there were no other choices in the back and that they were completely sold out. I told her that I definitely wanted it, but I asked how much it was.

She said the price tag said it was $80, but that it would be half off of that even though the sale had officially ended. So she tried to ring it up, but had problems, and so I asked her what was going on and she said that for some reason it was ringing up $27 with tax instead of $40 before tax. So after a couple of more attempts, she said, she would sell it to me for $27.

God told me that if I waited I would get it cheaper and that was the truth, as the cost of the watch went from $150 to $80 to $40 to $27, which was the average price of a nice Timex back in the pharmacy of our small rural town. Oh, and it was water resistant to 100 feet, but there are no lakes or rivers above ground out in our rural arid, dry, dry, dry area of rural Kansas. Does God have a sense of humor, or what? By listening to God the day before and taking a chance, or as some would say, a risk, God came through, and I was blessed and happy to have the exact watch that I desired. Thank you, Jesus!

Chapter 6: Processing

Some people spell Faith, R-I-S-K. Can you recall a time when God asked you to do something and you knew that if you did it, it would require a risk on your part? What was your response at the time? If you didn't do it, do you remember why and how you felt? And if you did do it, and it was indeed a risk, how did it turn out?

Spend some time right now and write out two or three things that the Lord has asked you to do in your life, and maybe you responded, "It is too big of a risk." Would you be willing to go back and try to do those things now? If it is not something you can go back and do, ask God to forgive you for not being obedient and then ask Him if there is anything kind of risky that he may want you to do in the near future. Write that, or those things, down. Now take time to meditate on Joshua 1:1-9, specifically considering what it means to be courageous and bold. The Bible frequently tells us simply to *be* bold and courageous, rather than giving us instructions to *pray* for courage.

Spend some time talking to the Lord about how you can be more courageous to advance the Kingdom of God and to see more signs and wonders happen as you listen closely to what the Lord may want you to say and do. Be open to not doing it the way you think is best. I would have thought it was best to buy the watch on Saturday, but God knew that Sunday was coming.

Watch for God's timely plan.

Transition

Transition is rarely easy. It seems like there are a variety of things that play on our emotions during any transition season. This could bring potential anxiety and stress into our personal realms and inhibit the flow of the Holy Spirit in our lives.

Back in 1995 while I was still a pastor in rural Kansas, I had driven up to Omaha, Nebraska, for our area-wide pastors' meeting. I was a pastor within an association that had periodic regional get-togethers, and this one happened to be in Omaha. While attending our event, a local pastor from Omaha invited me to a citywide pastors' gathering, and someone that I did not know came up and prophesied that I would someday live in Omaha. Since I did not know this person, I asked God for a Scripture verse to confirm the word. He led me to Jeremiah 7:7, which says, "Then I will cause you to dwell in this place, in the land that I gave to your fathers forever and ever." Now, my father was not from Omaha, so this was a spiritual application, as I was friends with three retired fatherly pastors in the Omaha area. Thus, I wrote *Omaha* in my Bible and forgot about it.

Four years later in 1999, while serving as a pastor in Dallas, Texas, the Lord spoke to me and said it was time to move to Omaha. I could not remember where I wrote the word *Omaha* in my Bible, so I had to search page by page until I found the verse. I shared it with my wife, and through prayer and the consultation with other pastors, we decided that this was a God thing and began to make arrangements to move to Omaha.

I let my church know of our intentions and put our house up for sale, but I spent roughly two more months at that church before completely resigning. All the while, our house did not sell. A local pastor then invited me to come to his church and help with a variety of ministries, volunteering to take monthly love offerings to support me. He told me that I had a position there while my house was for sale, whether it took two weeks, two months, or two years to sell it.

During the interim time, I began to look at Omaha in a variety of ways. I consulted with approximately five people that I knew there, but nothing opened. It just did not seem like a position was available. Finally, we sold our house to a couple who had been attending Christ for the Nations. They would be graduating in late May and wanted to move into our house at the beginning of June.

Since I could not find any opening for us to move to Omaha, I began to look elsewhere. Our search started with local opportunities in the Dallas area and then branched out to Houston, where we had previously lived for eleven years. As a result, we drove down to Houston two weeks prior to when we were supposed to move out of our house. I had contacted a moving company but had not yet informed them as to where we might be moving.

When we arrived in Houston, we first went to the north side of town, where Diane and I both had an interview to be on staff at a church. However, during and after the interview, I did not have peace about it, so we said we would pray and let them know. We then drove to the south side of Houston where we had previously been on staff, and the principal of the local Christian school offered Diane a teaching job. So we went house hunting and found a nice house very close to where we used to live in that part of Houston.

We made an offer on the house, which was for sale by owner from some nice folks who attended the nearby Vineyard Church. Then we went to stay overnight with some friends. All night long I could not sleep and did not have any peace about this house either. The next morning we went back and apologized to the people, stating that we just could not buy their house. We had only discussed this with them to this point and had not signed any papers, so they were kind and let us off the hook.

Then we decided that North Houston must be the place, so we ventured back up there and made an offer to rent a condo. Afterwards, we drove back to Dallas, glad that everything was settled. However, all the way home I kept getting this uneasy feeling, so when we got home I called the agent and backed out of the rental offer too.

The next morning I awoke very early and went out on our deck to pray. My problem was that I had seemingly looked every-where and yet had no place to move. Simultaneously, I only had four days until I was supposed to let the moving company know where we were moving so that they could schedule a truck. I was between a rock and hard place and was very anxious about the whole deal. So, at 6:30 a.m. out on our deck, I prayed one of those really spiritual prayers with one word, shouting at the top of my lungs: "HELP!"

God heard my prayer and instructed me to go to Psalm 46:1, which reads, "God is our refuge and strength, a very present help in trouble."

I told him, "You got that one right. I am definitely in trouble!"

He then instructed me to read verse ten, which says, "Be still and know that I am God." After I read it, He told me to do it.

I questioned, "What am I to do?"

He simply said, "Do that."

"Do what?" I asked again.

"Do verse ten," He said. He went on to tell me to be still and know that He is God.

I began to argue with God, telling Him that I was out of time, that I had to let the movers know where I was moving, and that I did not have time to sit still and think about Him. But He insisted, stating that I had been doing so much personal look-ing, networking, and traveling that I had hardly taken any time to hear His voice in the matter. It was time for me to focus on Him and be quiet. I continued to argue, but I knew in my heart that I had lost the argument and needed to comply.

So for the next hour I sat on my deck and tried to focus on God, without talking, reading anything else in the Bible, or worrying about the future. At approximately 7:30 a.m. the Lord told me to call a certain realtor I knew, and that she would have a rental house for us to move into.

This did not make sense, on many levels. First, if we were staying in Dallas, why had we sold our house? Second, the housing market had radically changed; it was a hot market with few houses for sale anywhere. In fact, after we sold our house by owner, we continued to get calls for weeks from people desiring to write backup offers. And the rental market was worse. I knew there wasn't anything out there. Nevertheless, I decided to call our realtor friend, and sure enough, she said she just discovered a new rental property the previous day and could meet us there in two hours.

We went to see the place. It was nothing like our home, but it was readily available. The bad news was that the owners were asking $1200 a month, while the mortgage for our home was only $950. On top of that, our home was in a beautiful setting and a great neighborhood, stationed on an acre of land, with two streams and much wildlife; but this rental house was in a tract home setting, with few trees. It just did not look that appealing.

Plus, the cost was way above what I thought we could afford, based on the love offering status that I was receiving from this local church. I did find out from the realtor that the owners were Wycliffe Bible Translators who were somewhere in Africa at the time, so I quickly prayed a prayer asking God what I should do. I heard Him say that we were to offer $1400 for the first two months, so if we moved, we could get out of the contract in two months' time. But if we stayed, the rent would drop to $1200 for the remainder of the lease. The managers of the house told me that they doubted if the owners would accept the offer, but they agreed to contact them on their cell phone in Africa.

After just five minutes, they came back and said that while they were surprised, the owners had agreed to the terms. So Diane and I, along with some friends and our son Jason (who was just eight at the time) began to move from our former house into our new rental house.

After we were totally moved in, I went into the fourth bedroom, which was my office, and prayed a simple prayer to God, asking, "Now what?" I heard in my spirit to call one of those fatherly pastor friends in Omaha and that he would know of a position for me. When I called him, he immediately responded that he had just met someone the day before who was at a certain Christian school in Omaha that needed a principal, teachers, and even a pastor.

Ten days later it was a done deal. We had been offered a job to move to Omaha, where I was to be the principal of an inner-city school and the acting pastor of the church's contemporary service. Diane would be the head teacher at the school, and our son Jason would have free tuition in third grade. Just one and a half months later, we moved to Omaha.

Chapter 7: Processing

Do you recall a time when you were in a transition and you tried to make things happen using your own thoughts, strengths, ways, and ideas? Did it turn out good, or would it have been better if you had prayed and received instruction from the Lord on how to make that transition?

What can you learn about trusting God with transitions? What Kingdom principle might you apply the next time transition starts to come your way?

I often say that trust is a must! What journey of trust is the Lord embarking you on now so that when you get to the next destination, you are ready for the challenges? Ask God to help you to prepare now for future transitions so that when they happen, you will be ready and can avoid the costly delays and confusion that I had to go through because I was not prepared.

Ask God to show you Scripture verses that you can begin to memorize and apply to your personal life for when potential change comes your way. Then you can hide those verses in your heart so that you won't sin against the Lord (See Ps. 119:11), and you'll be able to trust Him with those circumstances. Remember, *trust is a must!*

Chapter 8

Christmas

It had been a cold Christmas Day, by Houston's standards. Diane and I had spent most of the day indoors, sitting by our fireplace, and just enjoying each other's company. Around 11:00 p.m. I went outside, and there was a chill in the air at thirty-six degrees. I looked up and saw all of the beautiful stars shining in the cold, yet clear sky, and I imagined for a moment what the shepherds and wise kings must have experienced. Then I simply proclaimed, "Merry Christmas, God."

Within my spirit, I heard His voice say, "Merry Christmas, My son." Oh, the joy and wonder that filled my heart at that moment! He could have stopped right there, and I would have been satisfied; because prior to that moment, I could not recall a time when He had called me His son. This was one of those *wow* moments. I think the shepherds proclaimed that same sentiment upon seeing and hearing the angels. What else could I say?

But then He went on. He said He was going to heal me, give us a child, and give me a pastorate that would surprise me. At this point, I was in the middle of my third year of pain and anguish, being constantly sick with IBS (Irritable Bowel Syndrome) and other related illnesses. In addition, we were praying and crying out to God for our first child. And to be honest, I knew in my heart that I was not going to remain an associate pastor forever. All of this was wonderful news.

So there I was out in the yard, just enjoying the season and discovering one of those rare moments when the true meaning of Christmas is displayed. There were no artificial twinkling lights zigzagging up the side of the house, no dangling plugs with multiple extension cords, and certainly no reindeer on the roof. It was just the reality of a starlit night created by God so many years ago, outlasting the best manmade lights. And then, the best Christmas card ever came hand-delivered by the Lord. (Or should I say, voice mail delivered as a download from heaven!)

I went to sleep that night, thrilled that God had chosen to talk to me on that special evening. But the physical pain was still there, and while my spirit was blessed and secure, my body was hurting. But God was still good, and He had given me a specific prophetic word of knowledge precisely fit for my situation.

Three months later in March, Diane and I were praying and participating in a daily Biblical wisdom search. During this wisdom search, we would just read through the Proverb of the day, plus five corresponding Psalms in increments of thirty, and then pray for wisdom. So if today were the first day of the month, then we would have read Psalms 1, 31, 61, 91 and 121, and also Proverbs 1. On March 23 we read Psalms 23, 53, 83, 113, and 143, plus Proverbs 23. Psalm 113:9 says, "[God] grants the barren woman a home, like a joyful mother of children. Praise the LORD!" When we read that, it was like God was suggesting that Diane should stay home from her teaching job and believe for a child.

Diane had always wanted to be a teacher from her childhood. However, due to some strange things at college and another family marriage being re-arranged, we got married before she graduated from college. Thus, she had to take correspondence courses for several years before finally graduating. Because of this, Diane had only really been teaching for a few years, and she was really enjoying teaching at our church's school.

If she resigned, it would have meant a huge cut in our combined salary plus a cut in some health benefits, so it was definitely a step of faith. We decided to submit the word to our church elders. Since I was on staff as a pastor and an elder, it just seemed Biblically prudent and a step we should take. And since so many in the congregation were praying for me to get well and for us to have a baby, we wanted to include the leaders of the church.

The elders met, prayed, and discerned that it sounded like God, could be God, and might be God.

We then decided to take it to the school board of our church for similar reasons. After hearing our story and praying, they said it sounded like God, could be God, and might be God.

So, on April 3, 1991, we announced that Diane would be resigning at the end of the school year, believing for a child in faith. Keep in mind that most women resign either when they know they are pregnant, or just before the baby is due, but not before they are pregnant. This was a very large step for us. What would happen if she did not get pregnant? How would she feel? How would I feel? We had many questions, but we responded in faith.

During the week leading up to Mother's Day, we discovered that Diane was indeed pregnant. Because we had been keeping accurate records for the doctor, we determined that our little baby was conceived on April 6, just three days after announcing our decision. We were blessed to make the announcement on Mother's Day in both of the morning services at our church. All the people gave God a standing ovation for the answer to prayer. Jason was later born on December 28, 1991.

On June 1, 1991, all of the pain and symptoms associated with the disease I had battled for three very long years just suddenly vanished. So in six months, two of the three parts of the prophetic word God gave me on Christmas Day had come to pass. The surprise pastorate would come two years later, but I was just grateful for the gift God gave to me on that cold Christmas night.

By the way, Jason is now a young adult, and while I am writing this book, he is my primary editor. He has completed a one-year internship with me, traveling across the country and leading worship in over four hundred venues in many different states. He is enrolled in a local Christian university with a full ride tuition scholarship, and he strongly loves the Lord. But we would expect that, based on how God blessed us with this little boy who has matured and grown into a young man of God.

Chapter 8: Processing

When was the last time you prayerfully studied Scripture to see how God might speak to you through His Word? His Word is life to all who find it, and health to all their bones (Prov. 4:22), and He is the same yesterday, today, and forever (Heb. 13:8). He wants to speak to you. Take time right now to open your Bible, and ask God to show you a verse or point out a section of Scripture to read. Then as you read it, write down on paper or in a journal anything that you see that pertains to things you are presently dealing with. I believe God will show you something significant in His Word that will encourage you, enable you, and perhaps also challenge you to walk in faith and victory.

Then, go someplace quiet—perhaps outside if it is appropriate. Look up into the sky, and just say, "Hello, God." And then listen!

Chapter 9

Creation

I went for a stroll down a solitary one-lane road in the Texas Hill Country. The air was sweltering, and only the parched ground due to weeks without rain seemed to override the intense heat of the day. I was glad I remembered to bring my water bottle. As I walked, I took notice of many items in God's Creation, first and foremost the extreme quiet of the surroundings. Only my footsteps and the occasional wind gust made any noise that marked my hearing. It was so different from the city: peaceful, quiet, and then very quiet, except for the distant braying of a calf. It was refreshingly quiet, with many opportunities to celebrate nature. I chose not to speak.

I was alone in a land of sagebrush, hay, mighty oaks and pecan trees, and an occasional Texas wildflower. It was a wonder to me that those flowers even lived in the midst of such arid and thirsty conditions. I paused occasionally to ponder what their significance was. The sight of purple, yellow, and blue, demonstrating their hue, was a significant contrast in the midst of browns and tans.

It was one of those days when the sky was dotted by big, puffy, white clouds that looked like giant pillows floating in the air. I paused, remembering the day before when I flew above those clouds and wondered what it would be like to see them from below. Now I knew.

The weeds on the side of the road had recently been mowed, and they smelled like fresh hay. Some new grass blades had grown several inches above the rest, reminding me of the kind of grass that a pioneer might have used as a toothpick. The landscape at this point was broken up by round hay bales, scrub trees, numerous cacti, and a couple of antique, broken-down, weather-torn barns.

As I walked, I came across some lifeless bones that appeared to still have some flesh on them. Then, as I looked across the lane, I noticed the dead carcass of an armadillo. Perhaps it had been hit on the road. Whatever the cause of death, it was a poignant reminder of the lonely in the world who live and die without many or any friends, and who have never met a friend like Jesus. Although the armadillo really had little intrinsic value, I was saddened by this loss of life. I suspect our heavenly Father was sad too.

My walk continued on a road sprinkled with grass and weeds that were fighting for space in the cracks of the blacktop. Why would grass try to grow there? What would be the purpose? Would there be any significance in cracks filled with substance? As I appraised this, I began to realize that Jesus also wanted to fill the cracks of my life with His loving presence so that I might become whole. The weeds in the cracks on the road had become my treasury of significance.

Twice, I had to move off the road to allow an occasional car to pass. Each time I did so, prickly stickers clung to my socks in what seemed like an attempt to flee from their hiding places and escape to something different. I wondered how many times I have tried to flee my surroundings, only to discover that they were the set times and places that God had ordained for me in that season. I was further grateful for the times others had assisted me in my quest for something new and different. I decided to let the stickers ride with me back to my dwelling place. Even though each step brought slight scraping and itching to my ankles, it just seemed like the appropriate thing to do. After all, God had created those little seeds too. The least I could do was help them find a new home.

While ministering that weekend, I remembered my walk and tried to help people find the path to a new friend in Jesus and a new home in the Kingdom. The prayer sessions were filled with the Lord's presence. Several responded to God and began to blossom like the wild flowers in the midst of their weeds and concerns. This fine group of country folk loved Jesus and really wanted to serve the God of creation in their neck of the woods. They were so receptive to the teachings on the Kingdom, and many came up to me with the same earnest request: "Please come back!"

The healing service was quite timely. Several experienced healing, including one man who had gout in his arm. Others shared testimonies of healing from my previous visit there earlier in the year. The quiet assurance of God's presence was a reminder of the quiet beauty on the prairie road.

In my free time, I ate and fellowshipped with this small group of German and Swedish Lutherans. I even did a small, three-hour service project by trimming thirty-seven trees (mostly wild pepper trees, cedars, and hackberries) on my host's property. All the while, I carefully watched for snakes and scorpions, and God was faithful to protect me.

On a happy note for the farmers and ranchers, it rained during my last night there. The flowers on the road were also happy. When I was there several months earlier, God had me share a prophecy that it would rain by Thursday. Several people told me that this particular word was accurate in that it rained on Tuesday and Wednesday of that week. It now appeared to me that God had been reigning on the members of this church for about two years since their new minister, a dear friend of mine, came to be their pastor.

Through this experience, I have come to realize that I am still learning. I am paying more attention to my spiritual landscape. Some of it is dry, while other parts of it are speckled with occasional wild flowers. That gives me hope that perhaps my garden is still growing and will soon flourish.

Will you join me on my next walk?

Chapter 9: Processing

How do you see and hear God in nature? Have you experienced some significant times when you knew God was right there in that scene with you? What was the setting? Were there factors that led you to be more open in nature prior to arriving? Do you think that God uses nature to commune with us? Think about a really special time in a natural setting that was particularly meaningful to you. How did that experience shape you or change you?

Now pray and ask God to continue to release nature to you that promotes times of closeness with Him. Ask God to help you keep your eyes focused on the natural landscape so that you can then encounter the spiritual landscape. Also, consider devoting some time each week to be in nature in some way that enhances your walk with the Lord. Then, journal about your experiences so you can share them and have them as lasting memories of how God has worked in your life.

Chapter 10

Dung

When I was a pastor in Kansas, I attended a conference in Oklahoma City with a friend of mine from our church. We were also able to view the place where the Oklahoma City bombing had occurred just a few weeks prior.

On our way home, we were driving west on Interstate Forty. There was a southerly wind blowing that day, and the temperature was probably in the mid-seventies. I was driving, my friend was in the passenger seat, and we both had the car windows down. (Since I enjoy fresh air, I would much prefer an open window when the weather is conducive.)

About halfway home, I heard the Lord tell me to put my window up; so after briefly looking around for any potential danger, I then rolled up my window. My friend asked me why I had done this, and I told him that I had an impression from God to do so. He then asked if God wanted him to roll his window up. I responded, "No, just mine."

So we continued on for a bit. I could see in my rearview mirror that a semi truck was rapidly approaching from behind us and was moving over to pass us. As the truck came more fully into view, I could see that it was a cattle truck, which was a common sight in our part of Kansas and this part of Oklahoma.

When the truck passed me, one of the cows had what I can only describe as a *discharge*. That discharge connected with the southerly breeze that was blowing that day and landed squarely on my closed window. It was the worst green, slimy substance that I had ever seen so close up! It was dripping and oozing down my window, and in seconds it completely covered my entire window so that I could not see out of it at all. We pulled over to the side of the road, and I could not even open my door because of the amount of slime.

I can only imagine what would have happened at sixty-five miles per hour if that green substance had hit me in the face. This story would most likely have been told in an obituary! But God was gracious and warned me about it in advance. We had to pull off at the next town and go to a self-serve car wash, where my friend used the carwash to get the car clean so that we could roll down the window and drive in comfort.

Another time, I was driving in Texas and felt like the Lord said to slow down. While the speed limit on this two-lane highway was fifty-five, I dropped my speed to around thirty miles per hour. A truck then passed from the opposite direction. As it did, a rock flew out of the back of the truck and hit my windshield, causing it to crack in several directions all at once. I believe that the Lord spared me from certain danger and/or what could have been a much worse scenario at fifty-five miles per hour, rather than the slower speed.

And still another time here in the Omaha area, I was traveling home on a four-lane highway. As I was coming up a hill to a traffic light that was about a quarter of a mile away, I saw two semi trucks in the right lane. I knew that the light could soon change and that trucks take off slowly, especially on a hill, so I started to move to the left lane to pass them. But the Lord said to stay in that lane and I would actually proceed quicker, so I made a fast decision to remain there. As I did, both semi trucks moved to the left lane, and I went straight past them on the right. I looked in my rearview mirror to see if they were turning left at the signal, but they just continued in the left lane for no apparent reason.

All of these stories illustrate the great care and wonderful ways in which God will watch out for us if we will simply listen and respond. He is interested in our lives and wants to bless us in numerous ways, but we need to learn to recognize His voice promptly, without hesitation. When we do that, God will certainly provide us with great opportunities and avenues of safety.

Chapter 10: Processing

What is it about listening to Jesus that scares us? Why don't people want to recognize and walk in a place of hearing from God, even in the small things of life? Jesus said in John 10:10 that He came so that we might enjoy life and then have life abundantly. I think the abundant life includes not being sprayed with fresh dung, don't you? What unnecessary messes could you have avoided had you listened more closely to God?

What aspects of your life have you not surrendered to God? Write down ten areas of your life that you are convinced that Jesus is not interested in. Then pray and ask God to show you how He wants to take care of those things and do even more (see Eph. 3:20-21).

Spend time reading and researching in your concordance when Jesus spent time with people handling small things. Especially notice the small things that later turned into really big projects, which would not have been accomplished without the attention to the small details. I'll give you two such stories to get you started: (1) Jesus multiplying the fish and the bread, and (2) Jesus asking the Samaritan woman for a cup of water (see Chapter 1).

Chapter 11

Wedding

¡Hola! That translates to "Hello" in Spanish.

What a blessing it is to be invited to minister at so many churches in so many cultures! One particular culture I enjoy is that of Hispanics. I grew up in that environment in the San Diego area, and I love the food, dress, architecture, and style. Did I mention the food? Yum!

Anyway, I was speaking (with translation) and ministering at a local Hispanic congregation. I should have paid better attention in high school and college Spanish, but all I can really do is order a taco at Taco Bell. Do you want a sample? Just say, *"Si!"*

After I had ministered and taught with translation, I then was involved with prayer ministry. In that ministry time, I was blessed with a number of accurate words of knowledge that the pastor and other bilingual leaders in the church confirmed. There was also a number of amazing miraculous healings.

I came to this young lady who was in the worship band, and with a translator present, I began to share with her. I told her that she was dating the wrong guy, that he was trouble for her, and that she should prayerfully consider breaking up with him. If she would do that, then her old boyfriend would come back to church, get right with God, ask her out, and then ask her to marry him.

Well, this young lady had already been praying about breaking up with the guy because of some things going on in his life. Subsequently, I later heard that she did break up with him. While she waited, her old boyfriend indeed came back to church, got right with God, asked her out, and then asked her to marry him. And I attended the wedding.

Now, this testimony really includes a mix of *words of knowledge*, *words of wisdom*, and some *prophetic words*, too. A *word of knowledge* is information from God about a past or present situation with no prior revelation. A *word of wisdom* consists of insights and conclusions that help to solve a problem. *Prophecy*, then, is the foretelling of events that are going to happen. The tests for words of knowledge are based on the present accuracy of the word, but wisdom and prophecy are tested and discerned by the accuracy of the foretelling, and if it comes true.

In this case and all others, all I had was an impression and a thought. I still get nervous when sharing words, especially prophecies. My philosophy is that I'd rather speak and be wrong than not speak and be wrong. If I am wrong on words of knowledge and such, I am the only person who looks bad. But if I am wrong on prophecy regarding the future, I could really mess up someone's life. This is why we have to fine-tune our hearing to discern God's voice clearly and speak His message precisely.

By the way, when I attended the wedding of the young lady, the boyfriend she broke up with was in our city jail and had drug charges pending against him. God was good to supply the warning while also sharing the wisdom on how things could work out. Of course, the Lord has a history of doing that over and over in the Bible, giving us the basis of our faith. It is with that faith that we step out and allow God to stretch us. He just might use us to share important information with someone who could be in potential danger.

If the young lady had stayed with the former boyfriend, not only did she run the risk of being arrested too, but she also could be in danger of having all of her belongings confiscated. That is my understanding of the federal law when someone is arrested for possession of drugs.[12]

I mentioned earlier that all I had to go on was an impression, or a thought. Over the years I have been blessed to fine-tune my thoughts so that I more frequently am able to discern my own thoughts from those of the Lord. This is identified more clearly in the chapter entitled *Plane*, but I would like to add some depth here in this chapter as well.

Proverbs 3:5 instructs us to trust in the Lord with all of our hearts, and not to lean unto our own understanding. Do me a favor wherever you are (unless you are driving a car or flying a plane!): Lean over to the right. Now, lean over some more. Now, one more time, lean a bit more. At this point you should be very uncomfortable, because we are made to sit and stand upright, not to be leaning.

Our tendency is to lean away from God and towards the *beeps* in our lives. Then every once in a while, we hear some truth shared from the Bible, and we lean back the other way, thinking that we have made progress. Yet, our leaning is so distorted and we have become so used to leaning, we don't realize how far off-base we are.

In 2 Corinthians 5:9 we are told to make it our aim to be well-pleasing to the Lord. I am not a hunter, but I have shot a few guns, and a bow and arrow too, and I have learned that if the sight of the gun is off just a little bit, whatever I am shooting—whether a bullet or a pellet—will be off the target as well. At the point of the sight, we can be off just a little bit, but way down the line, we become so far off the sight, that we often wonder: *How did I get in this predicament? How did I get so far off course?* We have been leaning for so long and have gotten used to that lean, and subsequently our aim is also distorted. We have to struggle so hard to get back on the right course and to make up lost time and lost ground. Yes, the Lord is very willing to help us, but still the time wasted and spent because of unnecessary leaning could have easily been avoided if we had more accurate aim.

We are told many places in the Bible to have the mind of God, to think the way God thinks, and to act the way God acts. How is this accomplished? Well, reading this book is a start, but we must immerse ourselves in the Word of God. We have to spend time with Him, learning about Him, His nature, and His character. We must begin to lean away from the world and into the

Kingdom of God. We have to tune our ears to hear His thoughts and His voice when He speaks to us so that we are ready when He downloads a word to us.

Everything in the Kingdom begins with a thought. Let's take a look at 2 Corinthians 10:3-5: "For though we walk in the flesh, we do not war according to the flesh. For the weapons of our warfare are not carnal but mighty in God for pulling down strongholds, casting down arguments and every high thing that exalts itself against the knowledge of God, bringing every thought into captivity to the obedience of Christ."

We see that we have been instructed to take every thought captive to the obedience of Christ. Our thoughts have the capacity to destroy us or propel us forward within the Kingdom of God. God prefers that the Kingdom be promoted, so He gives us instruction in these verses to help with that process. But the enemy would like to destroy us and negate any previous work as well. So our task is to remain on course, speaking life and choosing the Kingdom of God over death and the power of the enemy. It all begins with a thought.

Years ago, I learned a little description of what can happen if a thought is not taken captive, arrested, and dealt with. It goes something like this: A thought becomes a consideration, and a consideration becomes a decision. Perhaps you get a thought that someone in your church doesn't like you. You consider this, and then you make a decision. The decision could be that you are going to do everything you can to defend yourself, even if it means tearing down the other person. Now, that thought will not promote the Kingdom of God, so it needs to be taken captive and dealt with, so that it will not surface again.

Anywhere along this path, you can choose to make Godly choices and Godly decisions. So as we continue, a thought becomes a consideration and a consideration becomes a decision—which in turn leads to an act. An act becomes an act repeated, and an act repeated becomes a habit—which ultimately becomes a stronghold. And what is a stronghold? It is anything that has a strong hold on you. So I say, let Jesus have a strong hold on you and your life. Psalm 18:2 says, "The LORD is my rock and my fortress and my deliverer; my God, my strength, in whom I will trust; my shield and the horn of my salvation, my **stronghold**" (emphasis mine).

Back in 2001, just after the attacks on what we now call 9/11, I was ministering at a church in Minnesota that very first Sunday after the attacks. I was scheduled to fly to Minneapolis from Omaha, but all of the planes were grounded, and we only had one car at the time. So the local pastor from the church I was to minister at drove down to Omaha, picked me up, and took me back up to his town and church in the Twin Cities area. I spoke at a seminar for them and then preached a message based on Psalm 61:2-4:

> From the end of the earth I will cry to You,
> When my heart is overwhelmed;
> Lead me to the rock that is higher than I.
> For You have been a shelter for me,
> A strong tower from the enemy.
> I will abide in Your tabernacle forever;
> I will trust in the shelter of Your wings. Selah.

Notice verse three, which speaks of a strong tower. In the message, I mentioned that so many were running from the Twin

Towers as they toppled to the ground, but that God would have us run to Him as He is our strong tower. He will not fall, crumble, or be destroyed, and we can count on Him in every circumstance in our lives. Even this thought must be firmly settled and rooted in our lives so that when temptations or trials come, we have made up our minds in advance and processed our thoughts prior to these possibilities. Ephesians 6 says in the passage on the whole armor of God that having done all to stand, we will stand. But we must take the initiative now. We must make the decision now. I like what Psalm 26:11-12 says:

> But as for me, I will walk in my integrity;
> Redeem me and be merciful to me.
> My foot stands in an even place;
> In the congregations I will bless the LORD.

Begin to make decisions that represent Godly integrity so that when it is time to make decisions and begin acting, your thoughts will be controlled by the Holy Spirit and not by your circumstances.

Let me show you more truth about thinking and thoughts. Turn to Genesis chapter one. God sets the pattern from the very beginning. In Genesis 1:2, we read that God is hovering over the face of the waters. The word *hovering* means to think deeply. So God is hovering and thinking deeply, but not much is happening. In fact the Bible is clear that it is not clear—actually, it is very dark, as the earth was without form and void and darkness was on the face of the deep. And we know that deep water is normally also very dark.

And suddenly in verse 3, God said, "Let there be light," and there was light. Wow! Or as my personal friend Ed Silvoso says, "Wow, wow, wow!" I like it when there is a suddenly by the Lord. I know it does not say the word suddenly in this verse, but the implication is there in that it really was incredibly dark. Probably pitch black. Extremely dark. Darker than anything you or I have probably ever experienced.

In verse four, I want you to notice that God saw something. What did He see? Come on now, I can't give it away. You were supposed to turn to Genesis chapter one. Okay, I'll give you the benefit of the doubt that you might be reading this somewhere and not have your Bible handy. Verse 4 states, "And God saw the light, that it was good and God divided the light from the darkness."

So let me ask you again. What did God see? If you answered the *light*, you really are only partially correct. Survey says: God saw what He said. I want you to catch this. God was thinking, but nothing happened; and then God said something, and light appeared. Then God saw the light, but He really saw what He said. That's the way it is with God. He says something and then He sees what He said. Now because He is not limited by time or space and there is no twenty-four hours of time like we have here on earth, He sees things He says right away, whereas we may have to wait awhile to actually see it. He is the Alpha and Omega, the Beginning and the End. He is at both places simultaneously. That is hard to completely understand (and not a part of this chapter!), so I am going to ask you to stop and pray, asking God to reveal this truth to you right now before you go any further.

Selah.

Now that you have prayed, let me illustrate it with the wedding story. God said that the young lady was dating the wrong guy, that old boyfriend would come back, and ultimately they would get married. Everything He said He saw happened just like He saw it in Genesis 1:4.

In verse five we see the completion of this Kingdom cycle in that God named what He saw, calling the light day, and the darkness night. To summarize, God was thinking, but nothing happened; then He spoke, and something happened. Then He saw what He said and named what He saw.

We really have the same strategy in that we are thinking about God, and He downloads a specific word to us for someone else. We speak it, and it is confirmed and begins to manifest and be revealed. As this process continues, we often see it come to completion. We share that testimony with others about how God did this, and that testimony usually has a name or title associated with it to distinguish it from other testimonies that we are honored to share and give God glory through as we were obedient to respond to His voice being activated in our lives. Whew, that was a long sentence!

In the chapter entitled "$20," I wrote about becoming disenfranchised from the Kingdom. That often happens because we are leaning the wrong way, unto our own understanding, rather than focusing on the Lord and what He wants to do. We need a better understanding of what God is doing. Proverbs 4:7 tells us that wisdom is the principal thing, and in all of our getting, we should get understanding. You would probably agree that there is a lot of getting and acquiring. We get and buy stuff for our homes, our cars, our office, and our children. We get tons of mail, emails, texts, and other forms of communication. We are always getting information about something, yet are we really getting an understanding of what God is about and what He wants to do?

The word *understanding* is unlike other words with *under* in them, such as *understudy*, *underneath*, and *underscore*, which all indicate that there is something above and something beneath. But the word *understanding* really does not take on that same connotation. The word *understanding* simply means to stand in the middle of truth. Otherwise, every time you had an understanding, the truth would be above you somewhere, and you would be beneath it or under it and not fully able to grasp it.

The Bible tells us that Jesus is the Way, the Truth, and the Life. The Bible states that Jesus lives in us, and we live in Him. So when we have an understanding of something, we literally have the truth of Jesus living inside of us. We aren't beneath it, but rather we are in the center of it, and it resides in us as we dwell in that truth. We understand this because there have been times in our lives where we were reading the Bible, perhaps it was the hundredth time we had read that particular verse, but on this day, lightning struck and the heavens were opened, and the truth of that verse jumped off the page and hit us between the eyes, and at one time or another, we all responded, "Now I understand!"

Let me illustrate this further. In the New Testament, we are told in at least two places that we are not to be ignorant of God and His Word. The word *ignorant* is the Greek word *agneo*, which is where we get our English word *agnostic*. According to the dictionary, an agnostic is one void of understanding. God says, "I want you to have understanding, and not to be void of it." When you have a void, there is great darkness, like in Genesis chapter one above where the earth was void. God wants us to walk in the light, which is the truth. As stated in an earlier chapter, 3 John 4 says, "I have no greater joy than to hear that my children walk in truth." That must get down deep in our spirits. There is nothing of greater value or joy that God experiences than to hear that His children are walking in the truth: That they have an understanding, that they are not ignorant or void of understanding, but that the truth of the Word of God is deep down in their spirit and it then influences and impacts their lives on a continual basis.

Now we must add in one more component here. In Romans 8:1-8 there is an in-depth teaching that deals with life in the Spirit versus life in the flesh. This culminates in God telling us not to be carnally minded. The word *carnally* comes from the word *carne*, which means meat. Hence, chili con carne is chili with meat. In a sense, I think God is telling us not to be meatheads.

Some reading this will remember the old TV sitcom, *All in the Family*. Archie had a son-in-law named Mike who lived with Archie and Edith Bunker. And every time Archie and Mike had a fight, Archie would refer to Mike as being a meathead, normally following it up with the phrase, "You don't understand me."[13]

God wants us to understand Him. He knows that we are getting things and information all of the time, but He also knows that while information is okay, transformation is great. And we can get information in lots of places, but we can secure transformation in and through the reading of God's written Word, which we call the Bible. It's the truth, and the truth will indeed set us free.

The truth of Jesus will help us stand straight and move away from so much leaning. As we then begin to lean into Jesus and His everlasting arms, as the old hymn writers urged us, we will begin to experience His words in our thoughts. Our thoughts will become His words that will bless and encourage others as we recognize His words as being full of light, not void and dark, but full of life-giving light. This can indeed help others avoid a destructive future by giving them the *now* word of God for a situation in their lives. I believe we will see God use us in mighty ways, so let's begin today to lean back into His presence and make it our aim to be well pleasing to Him.

Let me conclude this chapter with two short stories that happened to me when we lived in Dallas. One morning I was at the local health club, and I met a man one morning and began to talk to him. During the conversation, I told him that I believed he was a pastor. He affirmed that he was indeed a pastor, but then he asked me how I knew that, and I told him that God had just told me that he was a pastor. He then asked what I did, and I told him that I was also a pastor. He stopped and then said, "I wonder why God did not tell me that you were a pastor."

Another time I was coming out of a Christian businessmen's meeting, and as I walked out, a guy rode up on a very nice motorcycle. This bike was shiny and kind of a copper, metallic color—really sharp! As he dismounted from the bike, two other men came out of the meeting and slapped down two tracts on this guy's seat and walked off. I guess they thought they had done something really spectacular for the Lord.

First of all, you don't touch another guy's bike without his permission! And second, if you want to share a tract with a stranger, you should at least strike up a conversation with the person first, not just leave it and walk off. How silly some Christians are.

Anyway, I began to apologize to the guy with the motorcycle and took the tracts off his seat and said, "You don't need these, as you are already saved." How did I know that? I had never seen nor met this man before. This was a direct download from heaven to me about this situation. And how crazy is it to leave a tract with someone that is already saved. We need to listen to the Lord more often, and act out of obedience rather than out of habit and methods.

As I was apologizing to the man with the motorcycle, he responded that it was okay and it did not bother him. I then said to him, "Not only are you a believer but you go to such and such Baptist church." Now I had his attention, because as I stated, we had never met. Plus, I had never been to that Baptist church. He wanted to know how I knew all of this, and I had an opportunity to explain to him about the power of God available to us today and how God wants to use us and speak through us to others. It was a great opportunity.

Again, as previously stated, Leonard Ravenhill wrote in his book *Revival God's Way,* "The opportunity of a lifetime must be seized within the lifetime of the opportunity." Often, there is a narrow window of opportunity, and like with Paul in 1

Corinthians 2:3 where he said, "I was with you in weakness, in fear and in much trembling," we too may experience our hands getting sweaty and our hearts racing, wondering what in the world are we doing. Yet, we have bold faith rising up, knowing that because we have spent time studying His Word, being in prayer, and listening to His voice, now we are ready for action and ready to talk to someone else as God reveals to us what He wants us to say.

I'll close with two passages that I have previously shared, including Galatians 6:10, where Paul authored these words, "Therefore as you have the opportunity, do good unto all men, especially the household of faith." As you have the opportunity. Look for those opportunities to do good unto all people, especially the household of faith. Finally, this passage in Acts 10:38: "How God anointed Jesus of Nazareth with the Holy Spirit and with power who went about doing good and healing all who were oppressed by the devil, for God was with Him."

I want you to notice two things. First, God anointed Jesus not just for the supernatural and not just with the power to heal and do miraculous signs and wonders, but God anointed Jesus to do good. We often miss that small and seemingly insignificant detail. This principle is taught at the church we attend, Eagle's Nest Worship Center in Omaha, by our pastor Jim Hart. It is the little things of doing good that really matter to God. He knows He can use you to heal the sick, and cast out demons, and disciple people to come to walk more closely with Jesus. But can He use you in the small things, the things that others pass by?

I had a guy tell me once that he wanted to travel with me and see and learn about what it is like to be in traveling ministry. But as we got into this discussion, I learned that he wanted a free ride, to sit around a pool, and have his way paid for, I guess by me. I challenged him with how I started and still do to this day, in that I look for ways to minister to pastors and marketplace folks and those in need. But his response was that his calling and anointing were much larger than that, and that he did not have time to go about his town helping others because he just knew that he was somehow above all of that. He wanted to bypass the anointing to do good.

The second thing I want you to notice is that as you flow and move in the anointing to do good and help others—and yes, see the sick healed and other manifestations happen—that God is indeed with you. You may think that He has forgotten you, or put you in the corner for another day, but I can assure you that if you will practice Galatians 6:10 coupled with Acts 10:38 you will quickly see and realize that God is indeed with you. The Bible says that one of God's names is Immanuel, which means, "God with us."[14] And He will stay with you as you make your aim to be well pleasing to Him, walking in His truth, staying in His Light, and helping others move out of darkness and into His marvelous light.

Chapter 11: Processing

Have you ever heard God warn you of pending danger or perhaps inform you of someone else who was in a dangerous situation? What was your first inclination? Did you heed the advice from the Lord, or did you hesitate and wonder? I know it is easy to push the hold button and hope that someone else will respond and kind of let you off the hook. But it could be that God is testing you to see if you are willing and prepared for your next Kingdom assignment.

Second Chronicles 16:9a says, "For the eyes of the LORD run to and fro throughout the whole earth, to show Himself strong on behalf of those whose heart is loyal to Him." You see, God knows we will make mistakes, and He is okay with that. That's why He sent Jesus. But He is looking for loyal people—ones who will conscientiously follow the leading of the Holy Spirit and respond in the direction that He is leading.

Since this chapter included aspects about a wedding, let me remind you of John 2:1-11:

> On the third day there was a wedding in Cana of Galilee, and the mother of Jesus was there. Now both Jesus and His disciples were invited to the wedding. And when they ran out of wine, the mother of Jesus said to Him, "They have no wine."
>
> Jesus said to her, "Woman, what does your concern have to do with Me? My hour has not yet come."
>
> His mother said to the servants, "Whatever He says to you, do it." Now there were set there six water pots

of stone, according to the manner of purification of the Jews, containing twenty or thirty gallons apiece.

Jesus said to them, "Fill the water pots with water." And they filled them up to the brim. And He said to them, "Draw some out now, and take it to the master of the feast." And they took it.

When the master of the feast had tasted the water that was made wine, and did not know where it came from (but the servants who had drawn the water knew), the master of the feast called the bridegroom. And he said to him, "Every man at the beginning sets out the good wine, and when the guests have well drunk, then the inferior. You have kept the good wine until now!" This beginning of signs Jesus did in Cana of Galilee, and manifested His glory; and His disciples believed in Him.

In verse five, Mary told the servants to do whatever Jesus told them to do. And then in verse ten, we discover that the master of the feast, and most likely the guests as well, thought that the best wine had been saved for the end of the celebration. The principle here is that if we are obedient and follow the instructions of the Lord, we too will experience the best wine, the best results, and the best productivity. We must not lean on our own understanding or think that we have a better answer. Rather, we must realize that if we take our thoughts captive and obey Jesus, the results will be fantastic as we walk in His will and discover that His ways indeed are better.

Pause and pray right now, asking God to expand your loyalty regarding your Christian walk. Admit to God the times when you have not been loyal, and tell Him in your own words what is holding you back and how you would like to improve. I believe God will begin working a new attitude of loyalty in you this very day, significantly demonstrating His Lordship of your life and your obedience to Him.

Chapter 12

Pain

At a recent Kingdom Encounter Group that we host, we had people from nine churches in the greater Omaha area, plus one couple arriving late from Sioux City to attend and receive prayer for major healing and peace in their lives. As I got up and walked across the room to greet them, I had a stabbing pain in my left knee area, and I immediately wondered what I had done, or if I had somehow injured my leg and did not know it. Right after I greeted our guests, I realized this was God trying to tell me something, so as I made my way back to my seat, I asked who had that same stabbing pain in their left knee.

An older lady and her friend had come in earlier and she raised her hand stating she had the pain in her left knee, like bone on bone, which was what I was feeling. I had her stand and come to the center, and asked a few others to join me as we prayed for her for about 20 seconds. Then I asked her how she was feeling and she said it was somewhat better. I asked her to walk across the room twice, and after the second time she was high stepping and her friend was affirming that she could not have possibly done that prior to that moment. I had only met this lady once before and had no knowledge of this pain. She stated the pain was totally gone, and when she said that, the pain in my left knee departed immediately too, so it was a symptom of knowledge from the Lord that alerted me.

I then asked if she had any other pain and she said both ankles always hurt too, so I asked one of the other men in the room (whom I had just met the day before) to come and pray for her. This particular man had a history of two broken marriages, drug and alcohol use, and in many circles, he would not be allowed to pray for anyone. But like the woman at the well with a broken past, God wanted to use this man in ministry. So he knelt down and began to pray for her ankles as we continued on in worship, and in a couple of minutes her ankles were completely pain free too. I followed up with her the next day and a week later and she was still pain free, so to God be the glory.

Some might say, *I don't understand why God would do that.* Well, if we have to understand everything that God does, soon we have a god that looks just like us. And others would say, "Why does God do these things?" I think Psalm 115:3 answers that with these words: "But our God is in heaven, and he does whatever he pleases."

At a healing service in a local Lutheran Church, I stopped and prayed for a man in the hallway outside of and before the service, and he was better when he actually walked into the service. I see no reason to let people suffer for even minutes or hours when we discover a problem, so I just stop and pray immediately now. Even in greeting times in churches as I meet people I frequently just stop and pray. Recently, one of our ushers was limping prior to the service, and I prayed for him. He was healed within five minutes, and the limp went totally away. Praise God for his faithfulness!

My point about the healing at the Kingdom Encounter is that if God had revealed the deep knee pain prior to the people arriving from their two-hour drive to get there, then I would have prayed immediately and most likely seen the results earlier in the meeting. But God knew that not only did the one lady need to be healed of the deep knee pain, but the Sioux City couple needed to see it happen to give them hope and produce more faith for the healing prayer requests that they had driven so far to share.

Chapter 12: Processing

Bill Johnson has been quoted as saying that the difference between my destiny and assignment is that my destiny is to someday go to Heaven and be with Jesus, and that's God's job. But my assignment is to bring Heaven on Earth, and that's my job. The Lord's Prayer models this with the words, "Your Kingdom come, Your will be done on earth as it [already] is in heaven" (Matthew 6:10, NIV, emphasis mine).

Spend some time seeking God's Kingdom and simply asking Him how you can access His Kingdom to complete your current assignment.

Chapter 13

Eyes

I was driving my family to church one Sunday, minding my own business and paying attention to the road, when God interrupted my thought process and said, "I want to use you to heal eyes this morning."

To be honest, my first thought was: *Not today, Lord.* We were new at this church and had only been attending about three months. Plus our church was hosting a special singing group that morning by the name of *The Katinas.* They were going to lead worship and really have a huge impact on the service. The last thing I wanted was to try to present something to the leaders for consideration.

Plus, I knew that our pastor would be busy with our guests, and I just did not want to intrude. So, I prayed and responded to God that if this was supposed to happen, I did not want to hunt all over the building for our pastor. Rather, I just wanted to bump into him accidentally.

We had intentionally come to the first service, which was generally smaller in numbers than the second. We were thinking that we would not be there for the more crowded service, knowing that it would be even more crowded with *The Katinas* in the house to lead worship.

Of course, as we drove up to the parking lot, we saw that it was much fuller than normal. So, we looked for a place on the side of the building where we had never parked before. As we got out of our car, our pastor emerged from a door that I did not know existed, and he walked right up to our car. I then shared with him the word about God wanting to heal eyes today, and he suggested that I be the one to pray for that.

Now, I was really getting nervous. Keep in mind we were new to this church. In addition, we were hosting a major, well-known singing group that morning, which meant more visitors in the building. And to be honest, I was just content to share the word, not to be the one up front praying.

The service started, and at one point our pastor shared my word, invited me to pray for people, and invited people up to receive prayer right near the end of the service. Several people with all sorts of eye problems got well. He then asked me to stay for the second service and to pray again. I did, and similar things happened. Multiple people came forward, and many were healed of problems such as dry eyes, blurred vision, tunnel vision, shooting starts, spots, and many others.

Then, on Tuesday of the next week, our pastor forwarded to me an email from a man who had visited our church. He had prayed on that previous Sunday morning that if this was the church he was supposed to attend, that God would call out eye problems and that his eyes would be healed. Well, you guessed it: He was one of the people who got well that morning from eye disorders!

But I want you to consider this too. I was driving on one side of town, and God spoke to me about using me to heal eyes. Then I prayed, asking God to have me run into my pastor so that I didn't have to hunt him down. Following that prayer, I literally bumped into him in the parking lot, as he came out of a door that I did not know was there. While all this was happening, a man on another side of town was kneeling down by his bed, asking God to have eye problems called out that morning so that his eyes would be healed. No one could have made this happen or figured it out. It was a God thing and only God could have orchestrated that.

Now, fast-forward eighteen months later. I was ministering at another local church, and I shared the above story. A man was there at the service who stood up and introduced himself as the man who prayed and asked God for the eye miracles. How cool is that? This occurred exactly at the right time as I was entering into a powerful and uplifting healing ministry at that other local church too.

One time while standing in the twenty-items-or-less aisle at Wal-Mart with only two people in front of me, God spoke to me and asked me to move to the line to the left. I glanced at the line and responded, "There are seven people in that line." God then informed me that He wanted me to move to that line. I argued with God, pointing out my time constraints and schedule and that there were only two people in line in front of me.

He then called me by my first name and told me to move. When

He uses my name, I know I no longer have any options, so I reluctantly moved to that line. As I stood in my new line, I watched more and more people get checked out of the line I left, only to have my line bogged down while they did some price checking.

By the time I got to the checker, I was irritated, and I told the young gal my plight. I stated how I had been in the shorter line, but God asked me to move over. The only reason I could think that I was there was to talk to her about some problem she might have and that she should just share it with me so that I could get on my way. I was not a happy camper.

She had this surprised look on her face, but started to tell me how she had just moved from Tennessee to Nebraska and that she and her husband had a new baby and wanted to find a church. Now I was really irritated—this time at myself for not trusting God. So I apologized and asked her what kind of a church she was looking for. She stated that she was Lutheran. As a former Lutheran minister, I knew lots of Lutherans and was acquainted with several of the Lutheran churches in our town, so I gave her some suggestions.

At this point, I felt led to offer to pray with her, but I could see the resistance in her face. So, I told her that I could pray for her without us doing anything religious like bowing our heads or folding our hands. I could just look at her while I prayed and she could look at me, and the customers behind me would just think we were talking.

After the conclusion of our prayer, as I was starting to walk away, she thanked me and watched me with her hands on her hips as I was walking away. I glanced back several times, and she was just standing there with this goofy look on her face and her hands on her hips while I walked out the door. Of course, I later repented for complaining to God and for not following His instructions immediately. It is amazing to me how much can be accomplished for the Kingdom if we will only respond to his promptings.

Chapter 13: Processing

Can you think of a time when God surprised you with an impression or a thought? How did you respond? Can you remember a time when God wanted to use you even though it was not on your radar to be used or to be considered? Why do you think God does this in our lives? What is the purpose?

Consider making a proclamation to God right now that includes an affirmation of your willingness to respond when God asks you to, whether it fits into your schedule or not, and whether you have the time or not. Just make that proclamation to the Lord, asking Him to give you those opportunities to propel people toward the Kingdom of God while making a difference in the lives of others.

Chapter 14

Plane

Let's return to the story that I started at the introduction to this book: The story about my struggle on the airplane.

At this point, I was seated on the plane, and I kept hearing the words, "Get off the plane—it's going to crash! Get off the plane—it's going to crash!" The voice got louder and louder, and the words continued to be the same: "GET OFF THE PLANE—IT'S GOING TO CRASH! GET OFF THE PLANE—IT'S GOING TO CRASH!"

I was praying big time at this point. We have all heard or read stories of people who decided at the last minute not to get on a plane, only to find out that it crashed and everyone died. But they were spared because they decided at the last moment to postpone the trip. We heard similar stories back in 2001 when some folks decided not to go to work that fateful day at the World Trade Center.

So I was thinking, praying, and processing as I continued to hear the same phrase over and over, when suddenly it came to me. I knew what to do and how to respond. When I share this story with groups of people in churches and schools, I often ask for a show of hands to indicate how many people actually think that I stayed on the plane versus those who think I decided to get off at the last second.

The moment of truth has arrived...drum roll please! Okay, it was not that dramatic, but I made a decision based on the Word of God—not my emotions, my thoughts, or my previous experiences with potential danger—but entirely on God's Word. I stayed on the plane.

In the introduction to this book, I quoted from John 10:27, which states, "My sheep hear My voice, and I know them, and they follow Me." It occurred to me that in all of the times that God had spoken to me over many years, He had never once shouted at me.

Jesus said that His sheep hear His voice. I was accustomed to hearing His voice. It has been stern a few times, and always loving and caring, but never loud or in a shouting tone. His voice was never condescending either, nor was it with any kind of condemnation. Jesus speaks with authority, but He also speaks with authority. Bet you thought that was a misprint, huh? His authority is based on the Word of God, not tone; and His authority is saturated with Kingdom life that is recognizable to any of His sheep who have become accustomed to hearing His voice.

Authority has the root word *author*,[15] and the Bible says that Jesus is "the Author and Finisher of our faith" (Heb. 12:2). An author starts with a blank page, creating words and phrases out of nothing in order to share a story, write an article, or produce a document detailing the subject at hand. For Jesus, everything hinges on faith. The Bible says that whatever is not done in faith is sin (Rom. 14:23). The Bible also says that God rewards those who operate in faith (Heb. 11:6). So Jesus authors and writes our faith. He draws us to Himself and begins to write His message on the tablets of our hearts, as 2 Corinthians 3:1-3 depicts.

As His message is written on our hearts, His Word begins to circulate through our spiritual lives, just like the blood in the natural circulates through our bodies from the pumping of our hearts. In Psalm 119:11 we read, "Your Word I have hidden in my heart, that I might not sin against You." We do not want sin circulating within our spiritual lives, because the spirit will then affect the natural. First Corinthians 15:33 states that evil company corrupts good habits. We don't want evil company or sin to corrupt us. We want the Word of God, which, according to 1 Peter 1:23, is incorruptible. But if we listen to other non-biblical advice, read things that are radically against the Lord, and fill our lives with junk that does not produce Godly fruit, then, when faced with an important decision (like whether to stay on a plane or not), we won't have the tools of the Word and life of the Spirit coursing through our veins. Thus, we most likely will make poor choices because of that ungodly influence.

Jesus stated in John 10:10 that He came that we might experience life and experience that life to the fullest abundance. So when faced with life's choices, I can then rely on the Spirit of the Lord to direct me based on good, sound Biblical teaching. That is much better than someone's goofy opinion of life and how it affects the cosmic radiance of the sun, while trying to fathom the deep expressions of the stars in their astrological influence, or something like that. I want something that is proven and that

I can rely on. God's Word provides the basis that I need to forge ahead and make good choices that promote good thinking, all the while establishing God's reign in my neck of the woods.

I remember once in Houston when I had a bad cough. I went to the doctor, and he wrote a prescription for me. After about four days, I literally was coughing my head off, or so it seemed. So I called the pharmacy to inquire if I had been given the right medicine or perhaps if there was supposed to be a delayed reaction and response to the medicine. The pharmacist told me that this particular medicine does not stop a cough but promotes it. I then called my doctor and was told that he wrote the wrong prescription. Hmm...

The Word of God will never steer us wrong. It is life, light, and truth; and it will accomplish that which the Lord sent it to do. (See Is. 55:11.) Unlike the medicine I received that had the wrong effect, the Word of God will be a perfect match for what we need. By hiding it in our hearts or memorizing it, we will then have it available to us when we need to call on the Lord for an immediate answer. I have had many situations where, because of my recollection of the Bible and the words contained in it, I was able to make decisions on the spot, with present assurance and later proof that it was the right decision.

On the other hand, when I have impulsively done things without consulting God and without remembering or studying what the Word said about those things, then I made some mistakes that cost me my finances, my spiritual life, my reputation, and other areas that were hard to redeem later. Fortunately, I also know what the Lord says about my mistakes, shortcomings, and sins: That I am blessed, forgiven, and surrounded with mercy. Psalm 32 states this several times, and I love how the whole Psalm reads. As I write this, a well-publicized trial just ended in Florida that had the whole nation watching, and the person being charged with the crimes was found not guilty of the major charges. But I must remember that each day I am also found not guilty, not by a jury, but by the King of the universe, whose name is Jesus. I am further reminded that His mercies are new every morning. Guess what? There is blood evidence too.

God is not just the Author of our faith, but He is also the Finisher. The word *finish* implies taking something to the end and completing it. Paul said in Philippians 1:6 that He who has begun a good work in us will complete it. God is in the process of completing what He started in us. We cannot give up and quit. Rather, we must allow Him to finish that which He started.

Since Jesus was a carpenter, the word *finish* also has an additional relational meaning that deals with making a piece of furniture shine with a luster that attracts the eye. A good finisher can indeed take a rough piece of wood and turn it into something so beautiful that no one would even recognize the original piece. The same is true with anyone's life that is submitted to the Lord. God can take the roughest person and transform him into someone totally unrecognizable from how he looked or acted at the beginning. God's power is amazing! His love is adoring! His grace is forgiving, and His strength is renewing. After all, in Acts 17:6 we know that His disciples turned the world upside down with the power of the Holy Spirit that they received.

So remember, as I stated in chapter five, God does not rest when He is tired, but rather He rests when He is finished.[16] God is working on your behalf right now. If you trust Him and begin to hide His Word in your heart, you will be ready when you hear a strange voice, and you'll be able to recognize what is from God and what isn't. Don't wait for the crisis, the financial setback, or the relational difficulty to get close to God. Press in now and discover how much He loves you. Forge your way into Him as He enables, protects, and loves you in the process and through every circumstance of life. His promises are forever.

Chapter 14: Processing

Take a moment right now and write down two times when you thought you heard God speak to you, but later learned that it was not His voice, even though you acted or reacted to that message. After you have finished, just ask the Lord to forgive you of those times. Apply His love and grace to your life, asking God to show you how to discern His voice better in the future. Then spend a few more moments asking the Lord how you might cooperate better with Him on projects in your life that He is working on. Maybe, just maybe, you will discover through prayer and Bible study, that God is eager to complete certain tasks and is waiting for your listening ear and eager cooperation. He wants to communicate with you. He also wants to promote and advance the Kingdom of God through you, so you can then help others have a Kingdom encounter.

Therefore, as you upload your faith in action, I believe you will begin a lifelong journey of experiencing consistent downloads from heaven.

Notes

1. "download." *The Free On-line Dictionary of Computing*. Denis Howe. 25 Jun. 2012. <Dictionary.com http://dictionary.reference.com/browse/download>.

2. Johnson, Bill. "A School of Healing and Impartation: Anthology." Bethel Church. Redding, CA. January 2012. Conference message.

3. Ravenhill, Leonard. *Revival God's Way*. Minneapolis: Bethany House, 1983. Print.

4. "Quotations about Goals." *The Quote Garden*. 18 Nov. 2010. <www.quotegarden.com/goals.html>. Web. 28 Feb. 2011.

5. 2 Corinthians 3:18.

6. Psalm 84:7.

7. Romans 1:17.

8. "Mendelson's syndrome." *Medical-Glossary.com*. 2011. <http://www.medical-glossary.com/definition/Mendelsons-syndrome.html>. Web. 28 Feb. 2011.

9. Blank, Wayne. "What Does Wicked Mean?" *Daily Bible Study*. 21 Sept. 2010. <http://www.keyway.ca/htm2010/20100921.htm>. Web. 1 March 2011.

10. Kendrick, Alex, dir. *Facing the Giants*. Prod. Alex Kendrick, Stephen Kendrick, and David Nixon. Provident Films, 2007. DVD.

11. Pitts, Michael. "When Heaven Touches Earth Conference, Day 1." Sermon. Eagle's Nest Worship Center, 13 June 2011, Omaha.

12. "Offenses that trigger federal forfeiture arranged

alphabetically by topic A-G." *FEAR Law Library.* 24 May 2008. <http://www.fear.org/fedstat2a.html>. Web. 28 Feb. 2011.

13. *All in the Family.* Prod. Norman Lear and Bud Yorkin. Perf. Carroll O'Connor, Jean Stapleton, Sally Struthers, Bob Reiner, and Danielle Brisebois. CBS Television City, Hollywood, CA. 12 Jan. 1972-8 Apr. 1979. Television.

14. Matthew 1:23.

15. Thatcher, Virginia S., and Alexander McQueen. *The New Webster Dictionary of the English Language.* International Ed. Print. New York: Grolier Incorporated, 1970.

16. Pitts, Michael. "When Heaven Touches Earth Conference, Day 1." Sermon. Eagle's Nest Worship Center, 13 June 2011, Omaha.